INTRODUCTION TO THE PURVA-MIMAMSA

D1880135

Owing to the antiquity and rarity of this book, certain pages are regrettably absent, and readability is compromised due to the blurring of the original text. If you possess any insights regarding the availability of these missing sections, kindly inform us. Your assistance is crucial in ensuring the completion of this significant work for the benefit of future generations.

INTRODUCTION TO THE PURVA-MIMAMSA

PASHUPATI NATH SHASTRI

GYAN

Published by

GYAN

Gyan Publishing House
5, Ansari Road
Daryaganj, New Delhi-110002
Phone: 011-47034999, 9811692060
E-mail: books@gyanbooks.com

Distribution Network
gyanbooks.com
India, USA, Canada, UK, Australia

© Publisher
All rights reserved. No part of this work may be reproduced, stored, adapted, or transmitted in any form or by any means, electronic, mechanical, photocopying, micro-filming, recording or otherwise, or translated in any language, without the prior written permission of the copyright owner and the publisher.

ISBN: 978-93-7447-533-1 (PB)

First Published, 1923

2nd Impression 2025

Printed at: Gyan Press, Delhi.

The book is sold subject to the condition that it shall not, by way of trade or otherwise, be lent, resold, hired out, or otherwise circulated without the prior publisher's written consent.

INTRODUCTION TO THE PURVA-MIMAMSA
Author: PASHUPATI NATH SHASTRI

INTRODUCTION
TO
THE PŪRVA MĪMĀṂSĀ

By

PASHUPATINATH SHASTRI

M. A., B. L., Ph. D. Vidyāsudhākara

Lecturer on Mīmāṃsā and Smṛti and Examiner
at the University of Calcutta

CALCUTTA.

1923.

PREFACE TO THE FIRST EDITION

Modern students of Indian Darśanas do not, as a rule, study the Pūrva Mīmāṁsā as a separate system. Grammar has its life-long devotees, the Nyāya and the Vedānta have their specialists but the Pūrva Mīmāṁsā is without any such ardent and enthusiastic adherents. The neglect into which it has fallen may be traced to three principal causes. The sacrificial system of the Vedas, the main theme of the Pūrva Mīmāṁsā, being no longer in force, it is thought unnecessary to study the Śāstra that chiefly deals with it. Secondly, the Mīmāṁsā is regarded as less attractive and magnificent than some of the other systems of Indian philosophy. Lastly, the doctrines of the Mīmāṁsā have been largely discussed in other systems; and, so, the student thinks that, by studying any such system, he will have an adequate knowledge of the Mīmāṁsā. As a matter of fact, it is only the principles of interpretation of the Pūrva Mīmāṁsā that still continue to attract attention, and this is so because they are in evidence in almost all the branches of Sanskrit Literature and are indispensable to the interpretation and proper understanding of many an abstruse and ambiguous text. This general and continued neglect has resulted in the growth and prevalence of various erroneous notions about the doctrines and character of the Pūrva Mīmāṁsā, so much so that even its title to be considered as a Darśana has often been called in question.

But, the Pūrva-Mīmāṁsā has the right to demand greater attention from the students of Indian Philosophy. The Mīmāṁsā and the Nyāya are systems that had their origin far back in the dim past. There is evidence that the Naiyāyikas, the Mīmāṁsakas and the Buddhists were long engaged in controversy with one another. We have not had the opportunity of ascertaining how the Mīmāṁsā doctrines were represented in the works of Buddhistic schools, but in the works of the Mīmāṁsakas as well as in those of the Naiyāyikas, the tenets of the rival systems have been freely attacked and discussed. The school of Navya (modern) Nyāya, the works of which throw much light on the doctrines of the Mīmāṁsā, owes its development mainly to its criticism and discussion of these Mīmāṁsā doctrines. But, however elaborate these discussions are, we cannot always rely on them for a correct representation of the views which are criticised and refuted. Apart from the fact that in the heat of controversy things are scarcely seen in their proper perspective, it is impossible to gain an accurate and systematic knowledge from garbled and imperfect representations. To kill two birds with a single stone is a feat which can very rarely be performed, and the student, who would pick up an adequate knowledge of the Mīmāṁsā while studying one of the rival systems, must not expect to have more than a nodding and imperfect, if not erroneous, acquaintance with the doctrines and principles of the Mīmāṁsā. If he is at all desirous of obtaining a thorough mastery of the subject, he must devote himself wholly to its study.

Quite recently, the difficulties that confronted a Mīmāṁsā student have been, to some extent, removed. Of the two chief schools of the Mīmāṁsā, we had the works of the Bhāṭṭa schools, while it was thought that the works of the Prābhākara school had succumbed to the ravages of time. Thanks to the unwearied efforts of Dr. Ganganath Jha, three important works of the Prābhākara school viz., (i) Bṛhatī, the great exposition of Śabara Svāmin's Bhāṣya by Prabhākara himself, a work which, unfortunately, is extant only in an incomplete form (ii) the Ṛjuvimalā, a commentary on the Bṛhatī by Śālikanātha Miśra and (iii) the Prakaraṇapañcikā, dealing mostly with the epistemological and metaphysical views of the school, have been unearthed. Besides these three books, some other works of this school have also been found. Of these, one, Bhavanātha Miśra's Nayaviveka, has been referred to in the present work. These publications have removed the complaint about the scantiness and insufficiency of the Mīmāṁsā literature.

European scholars of the Mīmāṁsā had another difficulty in their way. Formerly, Colebrooke's essay on the Mīmāṁsā was the only source on which scholars as well as students of Indian Philosophy had to draw for information. This essay does not contain a proper delineation of the subject and is not, therefore, fully trustworthy. Herein, too, by his book on the Prābhākara Mīmāṁsā and his translations of the most important works of the Mīmāṁsā literature, Dr. Jha, for the first time, gave much valuable information regarding the tenets not only of the Prābhākara but also of the

Kumārila school. In fact, Dr. Jha is really the pioneer in the field, and every student of the Mīmāṁsā must be under a deep debt of obligation to him.

Since the said publication of Dr. Jha, a few handbooks, etc. have appeared which purport to deal with the doctrines of the Mīmāṁsā. Unfortunately, however, these mark very little advance on the work of Dr. Jha. As a matter of fact, in most cases they are but echoes and repetitions of his statements and views. Dr. Jha's interpretations and views, cannot, however, be taken to be the last word on the Mīmāṁsā. The subject is difficult and intricate; the doctrines have been represented for a long time in several antagonistic schools in a number of ways and traditional interpretations are mostly lost. In these circumstances, it must be evident to everyone that there is much room for difference of opinion and much scope for research-work.

The vastness of the subject has compelled me to confine myself to a limited area. I have introduced here only four principal topics, viz., validity of knowledge, Ātman, God and Liberation. In dealing with these topics, I have always tried to be as independent in my judgements as I could be. Many new features will, I hope, be found in this book, of which the following may be mentioned :

(1) I have tried to ascertain precisely the claims of the Pūrva-Mīmāṁsā to be called a Darśana in a manner not to be found elsewhere.

(2) I have tried to show that many conclusions of Kumārila and Prabhākara which are regarded as the characteristic doctrines of the Mīmāṁsakas are only apparent conclusions, but in reality are nothing but protests against the views of the rival systems.

(3) I have tried to refute the belief that the Pūrva-Mīmāṁsā is an atheistical system, and to establish that the Mīmāṁsakas admit that God is the creator, is the custodian of the Vedas and is an object of worship.

(4) It has been concluded by my predecessors in the field that according to the Mīmāṁsā, Ātman is not self-illumined; but, I have tried to establish that the Bhāṭṭas regard Ātman as self-illumined and cognition as an object of inference, and that one section at least, if not all, of the Prābhākaras, holds the same view.

(5) I have tried to show, in opposition to my predecessors, that the Prābhākara view of Liberation is not the same as the Bhāṭṭa view but that the means of attaining Liberation viz., the combination of 'jñāna' and 'karman' is the same in both the schools.

(6) The Pūrva-Mīmāṁsā and the Uttara-Mīmāṁsā are believed by some to be parts of the same system, while others think that they are antagonistic to each other. I have tried to show that they respectively represent two distinct kinds of culture (purification of the mind and absence of worldly desires) of which one is preliminary to the other, that both Kumārila and Prabhākara indicate that finer ideas about Ātman, etc. are to be gathered from the Vedānta while the Advaitins admit the necessity of the Pūrva-Mīmāṁsā principles for present practical purposes.

(7) I have tried to show on the basis of internal evidence that the Uttara Mīmāṁsā Sūtras first came into existence and that Jaimini adopted many theories of the Uttara-Mīmāṁsā, such as the theory of the existence of non-corporeal Ātman, without propounding them separately.

(8) I have not touched any question regarding the treatment of sacrificial matters. But, at the end of the work I have added a dissertation on the application of the Mīmāṁsā maxims to Hindu Law. I have selected one case—the prohibition of the gift of an only son in adoption; and, I have tried to discuss it fully from the Mīmāṁsā point of view, as has not been done in any other previous work.

With regard to many difficult points, the advice of my revered colleague, Pandit Ananta Krishna Śāstrī has been of incalculable help to me. Pandit Ananta Krishna Śāstrī possesses a thorough mastery of both the Pūrva-Mīmāṁsā and the Uttara Mīmāṁsā, and is entitled to be appealed to on questions connected with either of the systems. My best and sincerest thanks are, therefore, due to him. My thanks are also due to Mr. Patanjali Bhattacharya B. A. for his correcting the proofs of almost the whole book excepting the first few pages.

As I could not find a well furnished printing press, the printing of the book has not been, inspite of all my care, satisfactory. Sanskrit words could not be got transliterated. I have affixed a list of errors but I do not hope that it covers all the printing mistakes. In the transliteration of certain Sanskrit words, I have used ā for आ and ṛ for ऋ.

Calcutta University
1st June, 1923

Pashupatinath Shastri

CONTENTS

view of the Śāstradīpikā—'nirvikalpa' cognition of Ātman admitted by the Prābhākaras—the principle of continuous cognitions; pp. 88–95. *Ātman as the basis of cognition :* the doctrine of Tripuṭībhāna and Vijñānavāda—Tripuṭībhāna not preached by the older school of Prābhākaras–Murāri Miśra's view, the third course; pp. 95–100. *The Prābhākara view further investigated :* According to the old school, cognition is a mather of inference—the meaning of Saṁvit—some texts of Bṛhatī–Saṁvedya and Prameya–Prabhākara's regard for the Vedānta doctrines—conclusions; pp. 100–108. *Ātman is eternal;* pp. 108–110. *Ātman is omnipresent :* different views regarding the form of Ātman contrasted—the doctrine of omnipresence derived from the Vedānta-Sūtras; pp. 110–113. *Ātman as the agent and the enjoyer :* no real difference between the Mīmāṁsakas and the Advaitins—Why Kumārila describes Upaniṣadic texts as Arthavādas—Saṁsārin Ātman and Asaṁsārin Ātman–Advaitins recognize the value of Mīmāṁsā doctrines for practical purposes; pp. 113–121

II. God : no discussion in the Jaimini-Sūtras—Jaimini's view as gathered from the Vedānta Sūtras—God creates but 'dharma' or 'apūrva' brings about the enjoyment; pp. 121–127. Śaṅkarācārya refers to the doctrine of creation by God as one accepted in the Mīmāṁsā–difference between the views of Jaimini and Bādarāyaṇa explained; pp. 128. Probable origin of the tradition that ascribes atheism to Pūrva Mīmāṁsā—

significance of the Sūtra धर्मं जैमिनिः etc. pp. 129–130. Prabhākara and Kumārila erroneously represented as atheists—their denial of God is apparent only—God is neither the creator of Vedas nor has He any control on them—God's will plays no part in the matter of creation—He does not create for the sake of amusement but strictly in accordance with our actions—God as supervisor—the precise nature of his supervision; pp. 131–138. Kumārila ready to accept any doctrine which rests on the authority of eternal Vedas—his motive clearly explained in the Śāstradīpikā—a specific function ascribed to God—view of the author of the Prakaraṇa-pañcikā; pp. 138–146. *The body of God :* Gods supposed to have bodies—apparent identity of gods with their names; pp. 146–151. *God as an object of worship :* a cause of bliss—an inkling of the Advaita doctrine in the benedictory verse—Puruṣa and Īśvara are not identical—Mīmāṁsaka view adequately represented by Śaṅkara—description of god necessitated by injunctions; pp. 151–156

III. Liberation : Process of attaining it, Kumārila's view misunderstood—both 'jñāna' and 'karman' necessary—performance of duties exhausts past accumulation–experience consumes 'karman' that has begun to fructify, 'jñana' prevents future accretion—the opposite view of Bhāṭṭacintāmaṇi—'jñana' used in different senses; pp. 156–163 :

In the Viśiṣṭādvaita doctrine 'karman' regarded only as a preliminary—difference between

Advaita and Viśiṣṭādvaita doctrines; pp. 163–64. Prof. Keith's observations criticised—Vārttika passages misunderstood—a figurative statement in the Gītā—difference between the Bhāṭṭa and the Advaita views—a probable reconciliation—the process as described in the Prakaraṇa-pañcikā—no difference between the Bhāṭṭa and the Prābhākara views; pp. 164–171

What is liberation ? : the view of Pārthasārathi—the view of Kumārila assessed—his statements are not inconsistent—the Bhāṭṭa view agrees with the Advaita view but not with the Prābhākara view—agreement regarding the process but difference regarding the conception; pp. 171–75

Mīmāṁsā maxims and Hindu law : Importance of the rules of interpretation—rules applied to Vedic texts are applicable to Smṛti texts—Śmṛti texts supposed to have a Vedic origin—Dharmaśāstra and Arthaśāstra—authority of Mīmāṁsā-nyāyas; pp. 179–87. Adoption—a wife's right to adopt is a joint right—mother's separate exercise of the right under certain conditions follows from Smṛti texts—a bachelor or a widower cannot adopt; pp. 186–192. The sonship of an adpoted son is adṛṣṭa—an unseen merit cannot be produced in a thing prohibited—the violation of a prohibition causes sin and annuls the result—the Kalañja maxim discussed—distinction between cases of perceptible and unseen results—the Apaśūdrādhikaraṇa discussed—mere gift or acceptance cannot create sonship, sonship of an adpoted son different from ordinary sonship—an adopted son cannot be given in adoption; pp. 192–98. Vaśiṣṭha's prohibitory text wrongly regarded as a Paryudāsa—when a negative clause is to be regarded as a Paryudāsa ? : Two typical cases explained—distinction between a matter of natural right and one of Śāstric injunction—a negative text meant to check natural inclination is a prohibition proper—Vaśiṣṭha's text indicates a natural right—Niṣedhārthvāda Adhikaraṇa discussed—the point missed by Mandalik and other writers; pp. 198–20

The Hetuman-nigada maxim misinterpreted by several writers—the Hetumat maxim and the Saṁyogapṛthaktva maxim not simultaneously applicable—Dṛṣṭahetu maxim not applicable—Mandalik's confusion–the text स हि सन्तानाय not governed by the Hetumat maxim —it may be regarded as an injunction–all texts containing a reason are not Arthavādas—the text prohibiting the gift is unaffected in any case; pp. 207–215. The prohibitory passages of the Mitākṣarā—Puruṣārtha and Kratvartha prohibitions—the particular point of prohibition is to be judged—all the prohibitions not of the same character—the three clauses are prohibitions implied by Ṛṣi texts—prohibitions implied by restrictive injunctions as prohibitions proper—the same prohibition may be regarded as both Kratvartha and Puruṣārtha—conclusions; pp. 215–222

BIBLIOGRAPHY

I

The Bhagavad-gītā.

The Bhāmatī by Vācastpati Miśra .

The Bhāṣya of Śabara on the Jaimini-Sūtras.

The Bhāṣya of Rāmānuja on the Vedānta-Sūtras.

The Bhāṣya of Śaṅkara on the Vedānta-Sūtras.

The Bhaṭṭa-cintāmaṇi by Gāgā (Viśveśvara) Bhaṭṭa (Chaukhamba Sanskrit Series, Benares.).

The Bṛhatī of Prabhākara Miśra. (manuscript in the Library of Asiatic Society of Bengal, incomplete.).

The Bṛhat-ṭīkā of Kumārila Bhaṭṭa.

Gururājīya, com. on the Mādhva-tātparyacandrikā.

History of Sanskrit Literature by Prof. Macdonell.

Indian Antiquary, Vol. 1.

Indian Logic by Prof. A. B. Keith (Heritage of India Series).

Jaiminīya-Nyāyamālā by Mādhavācārya.

The Karma-Mīmāṁsā by Prof. A. B. Keith (Heritage of India Series).

The Laghu-candrikā (Gauḍa-Brahmānandī) by Brahmānanda Sarasvatī.

The Mādhva-tātparya-candrikā by Vyāsarāja.

Mathurānātha's com. on the Tattva-cintāmaṇi (Bibliotheca Indica).

Mayūkhamālikā by Somanātha, com. on the Śāstradīpikā.

The Mīmāṁsā-nayaviveka by Bhavanātha Miśra. (Manuscript with Pandit Ananta Krishna Śāstrī, Calcutta.)

The Mīmāṁsā-nyāyaprakāṣa by Āpodeva.

The Nyāyaratnamālā by Pārthasārathi Miśra (Chaukhamba Sanskrit Series).

The Nyāyāratnākara by Pārthasārathi Miśra, com. on the Śloka-vārttika (Chaukhamba Sanskrit Series).

The Nyāyaratnāvalī by Brahmānanda Sarasvatī, com. on the Siddhānta-bindu (Advaitamañjarī Series).

The Nyāyasudhhā by Someśvara Bhaṭṭa, com. on the Tantravārttika. (Chaukhamba Sanskrit Series).

The Nyāyavivaraṇa.

The Prābhākara Mīmāṁsā by Dr. Ganganath Jha (Published in the Indian Thought Vols. II and III).

The Pābhākara School of Mīmāṁsā—an article by Prof. Kuppusvami Śāstrī (read at the Second Oriental Conference).

The Prakaraṇa-pañcikā by Śālikanātha Miśra (Chaukhamba Sanskrit Series).

The Pūrva-Mīmāṁsā Sūtras.

Sanskrit-English Dictionary by V. S. Apte.

The Seśvara Mīmāṁsā-Darśana by Vedāntadeśika Śrī Veṅkaṭanātha (Conjeeveram.).

The Śāstradīpikā by Pārthasārathi Miśra, com. on the Jaimini-Sūtras. (Benares and Bombay Editions.).

The Ślokavārttika of Kumārila.

The Siddhānta-candrikā-guḍhārtha-vivaraṇa by Rāmakṛsṇa, com. on the Yukti-sneha-prapūraṇī.

The Siddhānta-bindu by Madhusūdana Sarasvatī.

The Six Systems of Indian Philosophy by Prof. Max Müller.

The Tantravārttika of Kumārila.

The Uttara-Mīmāṁsā-Sūtras.

The Vedānta-Kalpataru by Amalānanda, com. on the Bhāmatī (Nirnayasagar Press.).

The Vedānta-Kalpataru-Parimala by Apyaya Dīkṣita (Nirnayasagar Press.).

The Virodha-virodhinī by Umā-Maheśvara Śāstrī (a work of the Advaita school).

The Yuktisneha-prapūraṇī by Rāmākṛṣṇa, com. on the Śāstradīpikā. (Nirnayasagar Press.).

BIBILOGRAPHY

II

The Bālambhaṭṭi by Lakṣmī Devī, com. on the Mitākṣarā.

The Bhāmatī by Vācaspati Miśra.

The Bhāṣya of Śabara.

The Bhāṭṭadīpikā by Khaṇḍa-deva.

The Dattaka-mīmāṁsā by Nanda Paṇḍita.

Hindu Law by Dr. J. N. Bhattacharya.

Hindu Law by Mr. V. N. Mandalik.

Hindu Law of Adoption by Mr. Gopal Chandra Sarkar Sastri.

Indian Law Reports, Allahabad Series No. 14.

The Karma-Mīmāṁsā by Prof. A. B. Keith.

The Karma-Pradīpa by Nārāyaṇācārya.

The Manu-saṁhitā.

The Mayūkha, a Smṛti digest by Nīlakaṇṭha.

Medhātithi's com. on the Manu-saṁhitā.

The Mīmāṁsā Rules of Interpretation by Mr. Kishorilal Sarkar.

The Mitākṣarā by Vijñāneśvara.

The Nyāyaratnamālā by Pārthasārathi Miśra.

The Nyāyasudhā by Someśvara Bhaṭṭa.

The Prabhāvalī by Śambhu Bhaṭṭa, com. on the Bhāṭṭa-dīpikā.

The Pūrva-Mīmāṁsā-Sūtras

Raghunandana's digest.

The Śāstradīpikā by Pārthasārathi Miśra.

The Tantravārttika of Kumārila.

The Vaśiṣṭha-smṛti.

The Yājñavalkya-sāṁhitā.

INTRODUCTION TO THE PŪRVA MĪMĀṀSĀ

CHAPTER ONE

IS THE PŪRVA MĪṀAṀSĀ A DARŚANA ?

The word, Darśana, is derived from the root √ dṛś (to see). It ordinarily means 'seeing'. In its technical sense it means an act of seeing which is not tainted with any falsehood, or a correct ascertainment of something perceptible or imperceptible. To make it more explicit, we may define Darśana as an argumentative deliberation upon a thing of which some knowledge has been already obtained by perception or some other means, ending in the discovery of its actual form. So there must be some previous conceptions derived either by perception or some other means to make a Darśana possible. Without such conceptions mere argumentation will stand without a basis, and will fail to obtain the desired discovery. The inference arrived at after argumentation must again correspond to reality, for "there can be no formal correctness as opposed to real representation of truth............... For in the Nyāya view the knowledge that some S is P is not true knowledge which would require a knowledge of exactly what S were P".[1]

---

1. Keith, Indian Logic, P. 125.

The following verse states this view concisely,—"मानाधीना मेयसिद्धिर्मानसिद्धिश्च वचनात्", the correct knowledge of an object depends upon a 'māna' (means of proof) and the possibility of a 'māna' is due to a description. Here the second 'māna' undoubtedly means inference, because in the case of perception, etc , we can proceed without a description of the object. From descriptions or definitions we obtain conceptions of things and thereby we are enabled to start propositions. These preliminary conceptions are to be derived either by perception or by some means other than inference, for, if they also are to be derived by inference there will be no limit to arguments and we shall not arrive at any conclusion at all. The Śruti also says, "Ātmā vā' re śrotavyo mantavyo, etc.," ....where 'manana', i.e., deliberation is mentioned after 'śravaṇa', i.e, hearing. One should hear about Ātman from the Śruti and then by deliberation, etc., obtain a full and correct knowledge of it.

We shall now see how far this definition of Darśana applies to the Indian systems of philosophy. Brahman and Ātman are, as Prof. Max Müller has said, the two pillars on which rests nearly the whole edifice of Indian philosophy. So, if we examine how these two things have been dealt with in these systems and in what way preliminary conceptions about them have been obtained, we shall be able to form an opinion as to whether these systems should be called Darśanas.

The Darśanas are said to be twelve in number of which six are known as Āstika Darśanas and six as Nāstika Darśanas. The six Nāstika Darśanas are the Cārvāka Darśana, the Jaina Darśana and the four Bauddha Darśanas (the Sautrāntika, the Vaibhāṣika, the Yogācāra and the Mādhyamika systems.) The six Āstika Darśanas are the Nyāya Darśana, the Vaiśeṣika Darśana, the Sāṁkhya-Pātañjala Darśana, the Pūrva Mīmāṁsā Darśana, the Seśvara Mīmāṁsā Darśana, and the Advaita Darśana. We do not mention here the Sāṁkhya Darśana of Kapila as a separate Darśana, because it has been treated along with the Pātañjala Darśana as forming one system with it. It is for this reason that the Yoga-Sūtra-Bhāṣya has been described as the Sāṁkhya-Pravacana-Bhāṣya. On the other hand, we count the Seśvara-Mīmāṁsā as a separate system, because it differs fundamentally from the Advaita system. It establishes the worship of Saguṇa (qualified) Brahman, whereas the Advaita system establishes one Nirguṇa (absolute) Brahman. The Pūrva-Mīmāṁsā takes up the sacrificial portion of the Veda for discussion, and the Advaita system takes up the Upaniṣads; but the Seśvara-Mīmāṁsā system treats both of them together as forming one complete whole. So, these three systems may otherwise be termed as the Karma-Mīmāṁsā, the Karma-Jñāna-Mīmāṁsā, and the Jñāna-Mīmāṁsā; or the Pūrva Mīmāṁsā, the Pūrvottara Mīmāṁsā and the Uttara Mīmāṁsā; or the Karmakāṇḍa Darśana, the Veda Darśana and the Vedānta Darśana. As the Advaita system devotes itself exclusively to the Upaniṣads which are the Vedāntas properly so called, we can distinguish the Advaita system as the Vedānta Darśana.

The oldest available system that deserves the name, Seśvara-Mīmāṁsā, is the Pāśupata Darśana. The Viśiṣṭādvaita, the Śuddhādvaita, the Dvaitādvaita and the Dvaita systems are all of the same type.

Now, of these twelve, the six Nāstika systems do not admit the existence of God. So, if you take up the conception of Brahman merely, then these six systems are not Darśanas at all, judged by our standard. Let us next see how Ātman has been dealt with in them. The Cārvāka School conceives the notion of Ātman (body) from perception. It does not recognise inference as a means of proof, but according to it continued perception may be regarded as a sort of deliberation; and, therefore, as far as Ātman is concerned it may be called a Darśana. The Jaina and the Bauddha systems conceive the first notion of Ātman from inner perception, and then they ascertain various forms and characters of Ātman by deliberation. Some hold it to be as big as the body, others think that it is Śūnya, while others think that it is nothing but a momentary cognition, and so on. Hence, so far as Ātman is concerned they are Darśanas.

The Vaiśeṣikas and the Naiyāyikas have tried to establish the existence of God simply by means of inference without previously conceiving any notion of God from the Śruti or any other source. But to settle conclusively that there is one God by means of mere arguments without any preconceived notion is impossible. Hence, as far as the knowledge of God is concerned, these two systems cannot be properly called Darśanas. The Pātañjala system does not derive any conception of God from the Śruti, but it prescribes processes of Yoga which will make a supernormal perception of God possible. Though deliberation is not considered as the means of seeing God still it is included in the processes. So, strictly speaking, this system is not a Darśana, so far as God is concerned. There is this difference between the Naiyāyika, the Vaiśeṣika and the Pātañjala systems that while the first two hold that a true knowledge of God will be the result of deliberation, the last one holds that God can be made visible by carrying out the prescribed processes of Yoga.

The Pūrva Mīmāṁsā derives the first conception of God from the Śruti. It does not believe that the true form of God is visible through deliberations, but it holds that a correct knowledge of God is possible by that means. The Seśvara Mīmāṁsā derives the first conception of God from the Śruti. It holds that God is knowable through deliberations, and visible through meditation, etc. In the Advaita system the first conception of the identity of God and Ātman is taken from the Śruti. It propounds that the one real thing is visible through proper deliberations. Hence, so far as God is concerned, these three systems are Darśanas.

According to the Nyāya, the Vaiśeṣika and the Pātañjala systems the first cocception of Ātman and its attributes is to be derived from inner perception, but the true form of Ātman is revealed through deliberations. The Pūrva Mīmāṁsā and the Seśvara Mimāṁsā also conceive the first notion of Ātman from inner perception, but derive the first conceptions of some attributes of Ātman, such as eternal existence, transmigration. etc., from the Śruti. According to them also, the true knowledge of Ātman is to be derived through deliberations. The view of the Advaita system regarding Ātman has been given above. Hence, so far as the knowledge of Ātman is concerned, these six systems deserve the name, 'Darśana'.

Here we should ascertain the cause of the distinction between an Āstika Darśana and a Nāstika Darśana. It may be suggested that those systems which derive their first conceptions from the Śruti are Āstika Darśanas and those which do not do so are Nāstika Darśanas. If this be the cause of the distinction, the Pūrva-Mīmāṁsā, the Seśvara Mīmāṁsā and the Advaita system can without any difficulty be designated as Āstika Darśanas. Of these three, the Pūrva Mīmāṁsā shows an unusual ardour for establishing the eternal existence and an all-importance of the Veda and the other two systems are indebted to it for that. But a difficulty arises with regard to the Nyāya, the Vaiśeṣika and the Pātañjala systems. They do not receive any of their first conceptions from the Śruti; but they have still enjoyed all along the reputation of being Āstika Darśanas. Probably they are called Āstika Darśanas, because they admit the existence of the next world, of God and of an eternal Ātman. But there is no doubt that they profess to build their theories on inference only and indepedently of the Śruti, which, however, does not seem to be possible, as it has been wisely pointed out by Kumārila. In the Saṁbandhākṣepa-parihāra chapter of the Śloka-vārttika, Kumārila has shewn by strong arguments that the ascertainment of God by mere arguments, attempted by the Naiyāyikas, is absurd. It also seems probable that the Naiyāyikas and the Vaiśeṣikas have incorporated the theory of God as established by the Mīmāṁsakas into their own systems so that these systems may pass for Āstika Darśanas. But they do not declare that they base these theories on Vedic conceptions. The Naiyāyikas have also borrowed the theory of the perception of God by 'yoga' from the Pātañjala system; but that, too, has nothing to do with the Śruti. But their reputation as Āstika Darśanas is traditional. So, for the sake of the tradition, we propose to give another definition of Darśana below.

Any system which deals with sādhya (end or fruit), sādhana (means to that end), bhoktṛ (the enjoyer of the fruit) and God as phala-prāpaka (the ordainer of the fruit), is to be called a Darśana proper.

Now, all the six systems (the Nyāya, etc.) which are designated as Āstika Darśanas deal with these four essential elements and, so, according to this definition they can be called Darśanas proper. But the Cārvāka, the Jaina and the Bauddha systems reject the fourth element, viz., God; and, so, they do not properly deserve the name, Darśana. This is the cause of the distinction that is drawn between these two sets, the first six being called Āstika Darśanas and the last six Nāstika Darśanas.

There arises a difficulty with regard to the Advaita system. It aims mainly at establishing that there is only one Real Entity and so it seems to reject every thing else as false. It may be said, therefore, that the above definition does not apply to this system, and that it should not be called a Darśana. But although the Advaita system points to only one Real Entity, it does not exclude the consideration of all other things as unnecessary. It holds, on the contrary, that until the True Knowledge arises, the phenomenal existence of the world is true and that a discussion of all the four items is necessary as a preliminary to the awakening of the True Knowledge. Śaṅkarācārya has clearly stated in his commentary that until the True Knowledge of the self arises this Śāstra will continue to regard all manifestations of nescience as true. So, the Advaita system must be treated as a Darśana. The Advaita Darśana will, of course, cease to be a Darśana with the cessation of nescience; but until that time comes it is no less a Darśana than any other Darśana.

A doubt might arise as to whether the treatment of the sacrificial injunctions of the Veda which has been made in the Pūrva Mīmāṁsā at great length, really forms the subject matter of a Darśana. But this doubt will disappear if we consider the traditional definition of Darśana given above. Sacrifices are regarded as the means (sādhana) of the attainment of bliss (sādhya), and so discusions about sacrificial injunctions form clearly the subject-matter of this Darśana. These discussions are often very lengthy and full of numerous details, but the sacrificial system of the Veda is itself a very vast matter and any systematic treatment of it could not but be lengthy. The sādhana-element of the Pūrva Mīmāṁsā may be a peculiar one, but it is a sādhana all the same. And, so, there should not be any doubt regarding the consistency of the discussions bearing upon it.

A charge of atheism is also brought against the Pūrva Mīmāṁsā. If this charge be true, this system should not be called an Āstika Darśana in accordance with the definition given above. So, we must carefully examine the conclusions of the Pūrva Mīmāṁsā regarding God.

It is true that Jaimini has not discussed the concept of God in his Sūtras, but he has nowhere denied the existence of God. We shall show later on that though Jaimini has taken great pains for establishing that the fruits of actions are produced through apūrva still he has recognised God as the creator or the maker of these fruits.

There are two leading schools belonging to this system, viz., the school of Kumārila Bhaṭṭa and the school of Prabhākara. Of these two, the school of Kumārila is by far the more prominent. This school does not admit that we derive the fruits of our actions through the favour of God, but it regards him as the ordainer of fruits in as much as he helps us in obtaining them by creating so many objects of this world.

MM. Dr. Gaṅgānātha Jhā has observed in his famous article on the Prābhākara Mīmāṁsā[1] that Kumārila has denied the creation or the dissolution of the world as a whole. He has referred to four verses

1. Indian Thought, Vol. IV. p. 262.

of the Śloka-vārttika[1] as his authority, It is true that Kumārila has said that God, corporeal or spiritual, does neither superintend nor is the cause of this creation and that the creation or the dissolution of the world at any one time is impossible. But if we scrutinise the verses referred to above, we shall see that Kumārila does not at all intend to deny creation by God, but he intends to bring out the logical absurdity involved in the idea of the creation of the world by a God who himself-is a product of human imagination. Kumārila has written this chapter, entitled, Saṁbandhākṣepa-parihāra, not with a view to treating the problem of creation as such but with a view to rebutting the presumption that the Vedas have been composed by somebody, and particularly to refute the theory of the Naiyāyikas and the Vaiśeṣikas who first establish the existence of God by reasoning and then hold that the Vedas are a composition of God. He would rather have no God than a God as the author of the Śruti nor would he admit any authority of that Śruti which is a composition of God. So, if we properly judge the purport and connection of the above-mentioned ślokas

---

1. सर्वज्ञवन्निषेध्या च स्रष्टुः सद्भावकल्पना ।
न च धर्मादृते तस्य भवेल्लोकाद् विशिष्टता ॥
न चाननुष्ठितो धर्मो नानुष्ठानमृते मतेः ।
न च वेदादृते सा स्याद् वेदो न च पदादिभिः ॥
तस्मात् प्रागपि सर्वेऽमी स्रष्टुरासन् पदादयः ।
स्यात् तत्पूर्वकता चास्य चैतन्यादस्मदादिवत् ॥
एवं ये युक्तिभिः प्राहुस्तेषां दुर्लभमुत्तरम् ।
ŚV., सम्बन्धाक्षेपपरिहार, Verses 114–17

we shall arrive at a conclusion which is very different from that of Dr. Jhā. We find no reason as to why the creation and the dissolution of the world should be treated in a chapter where the personal authorship of the Vedas is the matter for discussion. The correctness of our conclusion is warranted by the very same verses of the Vārttika.

The simple meaning of the 114th śloka[1] which causes this confusion is : the assumption of the existence of a creator should be rejected as in the case of sarvajña. If in a book written by Buddha himself we find that he himself has been described as an ommiscient person (sarvajña) we can hardly trust that statement. Similarly, if the Śruti be a composition of God and if that Śruti says that God is the creator of the world we should not believe that statement.[2] Bhaṭṭa is not prepared to attach any value to that Śruti which is a creation of God, who again is a creation of the human imagination. He holds that the knowledge of God or his creation can be derived only from the Śruti (and from no other source) which is eternal and independent. Thus, we see that the intention of Kumārila is clear and that he does not deny that God is the creator of the world.

It is also a mistake to suppose that the system of Kumārila is not a purely theistic one because it has denied the existence of the physical forms of gods. But Kumārila has not actually denied the existence of such

1. सर्वज्ञवन्निषेध्या च स्रष्टुः सद्भावकल्पना ।

2. नर्ते तद् आगमात् सिध्येत् न च तेनागमो विना ।
दृष्टान्तोऽपि न तस्यान्यो नृषु कश्चित् प्रवर्तते ॥
ŚV. (Codanā)

an object. The truth is that he has not been very keen about this matter. All that he has wanted to make out is that we do not derive the fruits of our actions through the favour of gods, and that gods need not have bodies for that purpose. He has put forward the view that a cause and its consequence cling to the same basis. When a man has performed a sacrifice, the result will, as a matter of course, come over to him. Now, the results do not always come out at once, they may come out long afterwards; and, in order to show a connection between an act and its result two theories are generally propounded. According to one theory, the result comes through the favour of the gods who have been propitiated in the sacrifice, while according to the other an unseen merit (apūrva) arises immediately on the performance of the sacrifice which serves as a connecting link between the performance and its fruit. Kumārila adopts the latter theory. He says that if we admit this apūrva, the cause, the medium, and the ultimate consequence—all three will take place in one's ownself, whereas the favour of a god is not in the sacrificer himself, but is an extraneous thing.

Besides, in the texts of the Śruti there is no mention of the favour of any god. If any sacrifical injunction be properly construed, we shall see that it asks a man to produce a desirable result by means of performing a sacrifice. Thus, it is the performance that is the only means of producing the fruit, and as the performance does not continue up to the time of the production of the fruit, an apūrva is imagined as a link, and, so, the interference of any external god is not necessary. Moreover, the necessity of the favour of a god is not only not indicated in the Śruti but is opposed to its spirit. The Śruti tells us that the performance of a sacrifice is the cause or means of producing a particular fruit. If we now introduce the favour of gods as the cause of the production of the fruit, the importance of the performance as the cause will be ignored and this can by no means be the intention of the Śruti. So, there is neither any necessity for nor any advantage in introducing the favour of gods; and Kumārila has not, therefore, introduced it. Kumārila would have no objection to a god having a body provided that he does not interfere in the dispensation of the fruit. Thus we find all the necessary elements of an Āstika Darśana in the system of Kumārila; and, hence, it should be treated as such.

We come next to the Prābhākara school of the Pūrva-Mīmāṁsā system. With reference to this school also Dr. Jhā has observed that it denies the existence of God—"there is no room for an ultra-cosmic God".[1] If this system had really denied the existence of God we shall be compelled to regard it as a Nāstika Darśana in accordance with the definition given above. But before doing so we ought to ascertain the actual state of things. It is true that Prabhākara has not dealt with God as the founders of other Āstika schools have done; but this fact alone is not sufficient to establish the atheistical character of his system. Let us first ascertain the view of Prabhākara with regard to the Upaniṣads from which we derive mainly our conception of God. It is said that according to Prabhākara all the

1. Indian Thought, Vol. IV. p. 262.

Upaniṣad texts are mere arthavādas, i.e., praises; and, therefore, they do not convey any truth about God, etc. If we accept this view as true, the Vedānta Darśana which is entirely based on the texts of the Upaniṣads will be lost to the Prābhākaras. One might say that the loss of the Vedānta Darśana will not affect the position of the Prābhākaras; but the loss of such a system as the Vedānta is no trifling matter. And we shall show later on that Prabhākara has shown a great reverence for some of the doctrines of the Vedānta. As a matter of fact the Prābhākaras have not regarded the Upaniṣad texts as mere praises; and, consequently they have not denied the importance of the Vedānta Darśana. With regard to one Upaniṣad text at least Dr. Jhā agrees with us. We are quoting here his very words —"The Vedic texts speaking of the 'non-return" to this world cannot be regarded as mere Arthavādas.[1] Now, if it be once admitted that one text is not a mere arthavāda, it can no longer be said that other texts of the same class are mere arthavādas. It would be absurd to contend that some individuals of the same class are of one type while others are of a different type. So, we see that there is no reason for supposing that Prabhākara has absolutely denied the authority of Upaniṣad texts; and, consequently, there is no justification for the conclusion that he has denied the existence of God. In fact, there is no difference of opinion between Kumārila and Prabhākara in this respect. The Prābhākaras have denied the creation and the dissolution of world and the existence of the physical forms of gods etc., just in the same way as Kumārila has

1. Indian Thought, Vol IV, p. 258.

done. Hence, there is little doubt that their motive must have been the same as that of Kumārila, that they have tried only to establish that the Veda is not a creation of God and that the fruits of actions are obtained through apūrva and through no other agency. The following extract from the Nyāyaratnāvalī contains a passage which has been quoted from some work of the Prābhākara school which throws a good deal of light on the real attitude of Prabhākara—

निष्प्रपञ्चं ब्रह्मैव आत्मा, तथापि कर्मप्रसङ्गे न तथा वाच्यम्, उक्तं हि कृष्णेन भगवता, न बुद्धिभेदं जनयेदज्ञानां कर्मसङ्गिनामिति प्राभाकर-ग्रन्थगतोक्तेः ।

'Brahman who is the noumenal reality is Ātman; but we must not say so while we are dealing with sacrifices, for Lord Kṛṣṇa has said that one should not create a confusion in the mind of the ignorant people who are attached to karmaṇ,—this statement is found in a Prābhākara work'.[1] The author of the Nyāyaratnāvalī has not given the name of the work from which he has quoted this statement, but his own name carries sufficient weight and we can without any hesitation rely upon him. This shows clearly that the system of Prabhākara is not essentially an atheistical one. Prabhākara admits that there is God, but he does not enter into deliberations for determining the actual form of God, as it is likely to be prejudicial to the ordinary run of people who are fond of 'karman'.

In the Nyāyaratnāvalī we also find that both the Bhāṭṭa and Prābhākara systems have been recognised

1. Nyāyaratnāvalī, p. 60.

as Āstika Darśanas.[1] It is neither all probable that a leading theist like the author of the Nyāyaratnāvalī should have recognised a godless system as an Āstika Darśana, nor can it be presumed that he has called it so only on account of its acceptance of the authority of the Veda; for, in that case the Vaiśeṣika system which does not accept that authority would never have been included in his list of Āstika Darśanas. We can conclude, therefore, that the system of Prabhākara is a theistic one.

As regards the particular conception of God in the Pūrva Mīmāṁsā and his connection with the dispensation of fruits we shall speak fully in the chapter on God.

We have seen above that one of the systems of Āstika Darśanas, is called the Seśvara-Mīmāṁsā. This name may at the first sight lead one to think that it represents a particular school of the Pūrva Mīmāṁsā, and that the other schools of the Pūrva Mīmāṁsā, are atheistical. We find a typical work of this systems, entitled, the 'Seśvara-Mīmāṁsā-Darśana'. It was composed by Śrī Veṅkaṭanātha[2] about two hundred years ago. He was a follower of the Viśviṣṭādvaita school and wrote his work with the object of explaining the Sūtras of Jaimini. According to the view of the Seśvara Mīmāṁsakas, the Pūrva Mīmāṁsā and the Uttara Mīmāṁsā are not separate systems but form one complete system. In this work the Sūtras of Jaimini have been treated as supplementary to the Sūtras of Bādarāyaṇa and, so, the Pūrva Mīmāṁsā has been practically subordinated to the Uttara Mīmāṁsā. The

1. Nyāyaratnāvalī, pp. 59, 60.
2. A leader of the Viśiṣṭādvaitins.

Seśvara-Mīmāṃsakas do not admit an independent existence of the Pūrva Mīmāṁsā. Besides, the Pūrva Mīmāṁsā is known as the Karma-Mīmāṁsā, because it establishes that it is 'karman' only that produces the fruit and that no favour of any one God or gods is necessary for that purpose. But, the Seśvara Mīmāṁsā does not preach this characteristic doctrine of the Pūrva Mīmāṁsā. So, the two are completely different systems and the Seśvara Mīmāṁsā does not belong to any particular school of the Pūrva Mīmāṁsā. We have shewn above that the Pūrva Mīmāṁsā is a theistic system and that neither of the two schools of the Pūrva Mīmāṁsā is atheistical. So, the epithet, 'Seśvara', can by no means be meant for distinguishing this system from any branch of the Pūrva Mīmāṁsā.

It will be interesting to notice the relationship between the Pūrva Mīmāṁsā and the Vedānta. If we adopt the view that according to the Pūrva Mīmāṁsā the texts of the Upaniṣads are not meant to convey any truth, the whole foundation of the Vedānta would be gone. But, this view is not correct. And we have shewn above that even the Prābhākaras do not altogether deny the importance of Upaniṣad texts. Neither the Bhāṭṭa system nor the Prābhākara is antagonistic to the Vedānta; but, the affinity of the former is closer. The author of the Nyāyaratnāvalī bears out the truth of this statement :

'भाट्टैर्जडबोधात्मक आत्मेति स्वग्रन्थवाक्येन अविद्योपहितचिद्रूप आत्मेति सूचनात्, प्राभाकरेण स्वप्रकाशजन्यबोधाश्रयः चिद्रूप आत्मेति स्वग्रन्थे कथनात्..........................प्राभाकरो भाट्टापेक्षया न्यूनः'

'The Bhāṭṭas state in their works that Ātman is imperceptible and is of the nature of consciousness. And thereby they indicate that Ātman is consciousness covered by nescience (this is the view of the Advaitins). The Prābhākaras state in their works that Ātman is the basis of cognition which is self-illumined. ....So, the Prābhākaras are more remote than the Bhāṭṭas.'

It is on account of this close relationship that the Advaitins declare–'व्यवहारे भाट्टनयः' i.e., the principles of the Bhāṭṭas are to be adopted for all practical purposes. Most probably its closer affinity with the Vedānta has made the system of Bhaṭṭa more popular than that of Prabhākara.

We have, thus, given two traditional definitions of the name, Darśana, and have seen how that name applies itself to various systems. We have also noticed that the Pūrva Mīmāṁsā and the Uttara Mīmāṁsā are two distinct systems and that the former does not ignore the importance of the latter. We shall now ascertain if there is any distinction between a Darśana and a philosophy; and, if these Darśanas (and, particularly the Pūrva Mīmāṁsā) can be called systems of philosophy.

IS THE PŪRVA MĪMĀṀSĀ A SYSTEM OF PHILOSOPHY ?

The word, philosophy, has been taken to mean 'an examination of our means of knowledge' or 'an enquiry into the limits of human knowledge'. The structure of all systems of philosophy is based upon indepedent human reasoning; but, all the Darśanas do not stand on that basis. In some of the Darśanas at least the Śruti has been accepted as the infallible authority on many fundamental points.

The Bauddha and the Jaina Darśanas are entirely free from the influence of the Śruti and do not rely upon anything which lies beyond human reasoning. So, they are undoubtedly philosophical systems according to the true conception of the word, philosophy. There will possibly be no objection to calling the Vaiśeṣika, the Naiyāyika, and the Pātañjala Darśanas systems of philosophy; for, though they have admitted the authority of the Śruti they have admitted it in so far as it does not clash with reasoning.

The Cārvāka Darśana has a peculiar position. It is out and out an atheistical system and disregards the authority of the Śruti altogether. But, still it cannot be called a system of philosophy; because, it professes to accept perception as the sole means of knowledge and shows little regard for inference or reasoning.

But, the Pūrva Mīmāṁsā and the Vedānta can by no means be brought to bear the name, philosophy. Prof. Max Müller has observed that leaving aside the sacrificial treatment which is directly based on the Śruti and such other things, the Pūrva Mīmāṁsā has touched on many a problem which comes within the sphere of philosophy and that if the claim of infallibility in favour of the utterances of the sages of Upaniṣads be waived a real philosophy will be found in the system of Bādarāyaṇa.

Now, we must not forget that so far as the Pūrva Mīmāṁsā is concerned the discussions on sacrificial injunctions form the cream of the system. Here, Jaimini wants to lay down what dharma is and he treats the Śruti as the only original source of dharma. Discussions as to the existence and nature of Ātman and various other things are found here; but, they play only a very subordinate part. The performance of sacrifices (dharma) is the principal thing; and, all other things are introduced, simply because they are necessary for such a performance. The deities are necessary; for, without them a sacrifice cannot be completed. The existence of Ātman is necessary; for, if there be no Ātman, the enjoyment of the fruit of the sacrifice will be impossible. Had there been no sacrifice and no fruit to enjoy Jaimini would never have discussed the nature of Ātman. So, if the treatment of the sacrificial system be removed many topics will be simply out of place. Moreover, the discussion of all the topics which seem to be based on independent reasoning are really based on the Śruti; because, all the leading ideas, viz., the existence of the soul, its immortality and transmigration, the eternity of sound, etc., are borrowed direct from the Śruti; and, arguments are advanced not for the purpose of building up new theories but for supporting and developing the ideas of the Śruti. Strictly speaking, this sort of reasoning cannot be regarded as independent human reasoning. So, if the Śruti be discarded the arguments will lose their central plank and will consequently lose much of their charm.

The same remarks will apply to the Vedānta system also This system has arrived at conclusions regarding the nature of Ātman, Nirguṇa Brahman, etc., which can never be asertained by inference. The ideas of the Śruti are bred-in the bones of the Vedānta system and it is not easy to imagine how it can strip itself of those ideas.

THE PŪRVA MĪMĀṀSĀ AND THE UTTARA MĪMĀṀSĀ

The above two names have all along been used in many authoritative works to designate the two systems, the Karma-Mīmāṁsā and the Vedānta. A question naturally arises as to why they should be so called.

The Seśvara-Mīmāṁsā-Darśana regards the two systems as one; and, so, according to it, the epithets, Pūrva and Uttara, mean simply the former and the latter parts of the same system. But, if the two systems really form one work we do not understand on what principle this division has been made. We can not take the word 'jijñāsā' in the sūtra, 'Athā' to Brahmajijñāsā', as indicating the commencement of the latter part; for, the word, jijñāsā, is also found in the first sūtra of the fourth chapter of the Pūrva Mīmāṁsā, 'Athā'taḥ kra·tvartha-puruṣārthayor jijñāsā'; and, the latter part does not commence therewith. If we take such a sūtra as the title of a new work or part, as Prof. Max Müller has said[1], we should have here three parts instead of two. Nor, can it be said that the division is due to the treatment of different matters; for, according to the Seśvara Mīmāṁsā, Dharma and Brahman are not exclusive of each other. Dharma and Brahman are the the two principal topics which have been dealt with in these two systems. If Dharma includes Brahman[2] there will be only one main subject and not two. It is not also possible to take subordinate matters into account; for, then we shall have more than two themes.

1. Six systems of Indian Philosophy, p. 261.

2. अत्र धर्मशब्देन कृत्स्नो वेदार्थो लभ्यते, अतएव सिद्धपरभागस्यापि संग्रहः । Seśvara-Mīmāṁsā-Darśana, p. 4.

In the Pūrva Mīmāṁsā itself the first six chapters deal with 'upadeśa' and the next six chapters deal with 'atideśa'; but, no division of the Pūrva Mīmāṁsā has been made on that basis.

It may, next, be suggested that the division is due to different authorship. That portion, which was composed by Jaimini goes by the name of Pūrva Mīmāṁsā, and that composed by Bādarāyaṇa, is known as the Uttara Mīmāṁsā. In the case of the prose work, Kādambarī, we find just the same thing. Bāṇa wrote the first part; and, after his death his son completed the work by writing the second part. But, there is a difference between these two cases. Bāṇa's son completed his father's work because his father had died; but, here there is nothing to show why Jaimini stopped with the Pūrva Mīmāṁsā and did not compose the Uttara Mīmāṁsā. It is believed that he was a sage; and, as a sage he was certainly competent enough to finish the rest of his work. And, so, there was no necessity for his making over the charge to Bādarāyaṇa. Besides, this sort of division presupposes that the Pūrva Mīmāṁsā was composed before the Uttara Mīmāṁsā. So, unless the priority of the Pūrva Mīmāṁsā is first established this division into Pūrva and Uttara will be untenable.

Prof. Max Müller is of opinion that 'pūrva' does not mean 'prior in time.' He says : 'The names, however, were not meant to imply, as Colebrooke seems to have supposed, that the Pūrva Mīmāṁsā was prior in time, though it is true that it is sometimes called Prācī, previous... I should not like to commit myself so far as to claim priority in time for the Vedānta......We saw why the fact that Bādarāyaṇa quotes Jaimini cannot be used for chronological purposes; for, Jaimini returns the complement and quotes Bādarāyaṇa.'

Let us, now, see if we can obtain any evidence on the point from the sūtras themselves. In ten sūtras of the Uttara Mīmāṁsā[1] Jaimini's name is found, whereas Bādarāyaṇa's name is found in five sūtras of the Pūrva Mīmāṁsā.[2] It is remarkable that the matters discussed in nine out of the ten sūtras of the Uttara Mīmāṁsā are not found at all in the sūtras of Jaimini; but, the matter of the tenth sūtra only corresponds with that of a sūtra of the Pūrva Mīmāṁsā. This fact points to several inferences. It may be supposed that the Jaimini mentioned in the nine sūtras of the Uttara Mīmāṁsā is different from the Jaimini mentioned in the tenth sūtra, or that Bādarāyaṇa refers to some other work or works of Jaimini which have not come down to us, or that Bādarāyaṇa refers to such views of Jaimini which were not reduced to the form of sūtras at all.

The purport of the first inference is that Bādarāyaṇa has referred at least to two Jaiminis of whom one was the author of the Pūrva-Mīmāṁsā-Sūtras. But, it is not probable that Bādarāyaṇa has referred to more than one Jaimini. Had that been the fact he would have certainly given some hint to that effect; but, the

---

1. I. ii. 28	III. iv. 2	2. I. i. 5
I. ii. 31	III. iv. 18	II. ii. 19
I. iv. 18	III. iv. 40	VI. i. 8
I. iii. 31	IV. iii. 12	X. viii. 44
III. ii. 40	IV. iv. 5	XI. i. 64

name is mentioned in all the sūtras in the same strain without the shadow of a distinction. Hence, the above conclusion does not seem to be satisfactory. The second and the third inferences are virtually the same; and, they are to the effect that the same Jaimini is referred to in the Uttara-Mīmāṁsā-Sūtras.

Prof. Keith, however, raises a doubt as to the identity of Jaimini. He says : 'Who Jaimini was, I can not say, ...As an authority on philosophy Jaimini appears in the Vedānta Sūtras, and often in the later works; but, it is significant that while it is possible that the Mahābhārata recognises the existence of the Mīmāṁsā it does not refer to Jaimini as a philosopher but merely as an ancient sage.'[1] But, the Mahābhārata does not propose to give a list of the philosophers of its time, nor has it any particular occasion for naming Jaimini as a philosopher. So, the mere fact that Jaimini is not referred to in the Mahābhārata as a philosopher is not enough to prove that Jaimini was not an author of the Pūrva-Mīmāṁsā-Sūtras.

There is a long-established tradition that Jalmini, who was a disciple of Bādarāyaṇa, composed the Pūrva-Mīmāṁsā-Sūtras. We must not ignore this tradition unless we obtain some strong evidence against it. It is not absurd to assume that Jaimini was a worthy disciple of Bādarāyaṇa, that Bādarāyaṇa had discussed various problems with him and that at the time of writing his sūtras he referred to the views of Jaimini. Only one such discussion is found emdodied in a sūtra of Jaimini while others are not found. This omission may be

1. The Karma-Mīmāṁsā, p. 5.

explained by assuming that Jaimini did not like to embody those discussions in his sūtras or that he put them in some other works of his which are not extant. We are practically assuming here only one thing, viz, the possibility of the existence of some other works of the same Jaimini; and, this is certainly preferable to assuming that there were many Jaiminis and that there were many works of them which have perished in course of time.

It may appear strange that Bādarāyaṇa, who was the preceptor, referred to the views of Jaimini, his pupil. But, even in those days such a thing was not impossible. After finishing the study of the Vedas the student was required to study Mīmāṁsā. At this period the rigour of discipline would be relaxed and he could mix more freely with his preceptor. Śabara Svāmin has indicated this while explaining the word 'atha' in the first sūtra of the Pūrva Mīmāṁsā. The student used to be treated at this stage somewhat like a research scholar of modern times. The worth of a scholar like Jaimini was sure to be appreciated by Bādarāyaṇa; and, there is no harm in thinking that Bādarāyaṇa took his views into consideration. So, we see that the mention of Jaimini's name in the sūtras of Bādarāyaṇa may be consistent with the tradition. Hence, we may draw the conclusion that the name of Jaimini, the author of the Pūrva-Mīmāṁsā-Sūtras, is referred to in the sūtras of the Uttara Mīmāṁsā.

Of the sūtras of Jaimini in which the name of Bādarāyaṇa is found, the fifth deserves the greatest attention. So, let us first take this sūtra for consideration. If we carefully analyse this sūtra we shall realise that the name of Bādarāyaṇa is mentioned here not for the purpose of merely supporting the author's view, but also for expressing a feeling of gratitude to Bādarāyaṇa. This sutra does not contain the argument on which the theory of the existence of a non-corporeal Ātman is based, while we find it in the corresponding sūtra of the Vedānta.[1] This sūtra of Jaimini cannot be fully explained without referring to the aforementioned sūtra of the Uttara Mīmāṁsā. We shall see later on that Upavarṣa, Śabara, Śaṅkara and Kumārila are all of the same opinion. The doctrine of the existence of a non-corporeal Ātman is one of the principal doctrines of the Pūrva Mīmāṃsā; and, unless it is assumed that Jaimini had known the Uttara-Mīmāṁsā-Sūtras first, it will be difficult to explain why he should have only so slightly hinted at it in his own sūtra.

Mr. Nilkantha Shastri has made an attempt to prove that Bādarāyaṇa, whose name is mentioned in the fifth sūtra of Jaimini, is not the same person as the author of the Vedānta-Sūtras; but, he is a Mīmāṁsist anterior to Jamini. His arguments will be found in the following extract which is quoted from an article published in the Indian Antiquary.

'It is clear that there is nothing corresponding to these discussions or even remotely bearing upon them in the Vedānta-Sūtras. 1-i-5 is a case that requires a little more consideration; for, here Jaimini claims that Bādarāyaṇa and himself are at one on the question of

1. एक आत्मनः शरीरे भावात् III. iii. 53.

the eternity and infallibility of 'word.' It might, therefore, appear at first sight that at least the Bādarāyaṇa referred to here must be the same as the author of the Vedānta-Sūtras, who also maintains the eternity and the infallibility of the Veda. But, closer scrutiny shows that here again we are dealing with one of the most vital points of difference between Mīmāṁsā and Vedānta. In the view of the former the Veda's authority is innate and absolute and not dependent on any god or deity, personal or otherwise; the Vedāntist view is that the eternity of the Veda is only a relative quality and dependent on Īśvara. Hence, we find that the reason assigned by the Mimaṁsist for his position is अनपेक्षत्वात्, while the reasons assigned by Bādarāyaṇa in Vedānta-Sūtra 1.iii. 28, are अतः प्रभवात् प्रत्यक्षानुमानाभ्याम्. And, it is to be particularly noticed that Śaṅkara repeats part of the sūtra of Jaimini 1-i-5 above, औत्पत्तिकस्तु etc., in the pūrvapakṣa. In his comment on the Vedānta-Sūtra just referred to, Śaṅkara must surely have noticed that a Bādarāyaṇa is referred to as taking Jaimini's view in the औत्पत्तिक sūtra; and, if he believed for a moment that it was his own Sūtrakāra who was so mentioned, it is not in the least likely that he would have treated the very sūtra of Jaimini as the pūrvapakṣa view to be refuted by him. On the contrary, we should find Śaṅkara attempting somehow a reconciliation between the contrary view of Bādarāyaṇa, the one mentioned by Jaimini and the other stated in the Vedānta-Sūtra. To my mind this fact taken along with the other that in the remaining four instances where Bādarāyaṇa is referred to by Jaimini there is nothing to suggest an identity with the author of the Vedānta-

Sūtras, is conclusive proof that the Bādarāyaṇa referred to by Jaimini, is anterior to him and is a Mimāṁsist different from the author of the Vedānta-Sūtras.'[1]

The first argument adduced by Mr. Shastri is that as the Mīmāṁsist view of the eternity of the Veda is different from the Vedāntist view, the Sūtrakāras of the two systems cannot be at one on that point. Mr. Shastri has not cited any authority in support of this statement. So far as we know, this does not seem to be a correct representation. We shall show in the chapter on God that in the view of the Mīmāṁsakas the Vedas are regarded as uncreated just in the same manner as by the Vedāntis. The Vedāntin never admits that God or any other deity has any independent control over the Vedas. This view has been expressly stated in the Bhāmatī in the Śāstra-yonitva adhikaraṇa. We quote here the very words of the Bhāmatī :—"पुरुषास्वातन्त्र्यमात्रमपौरुषेयत्वं रोचयन्त जैमिनीया अपि तच्च अस्माकमपि समानम्, 'the followers of Jaimini also mean by अपौरुषेयत्व nothing more than the want of independent control on the part of God; we too, hold the same view'. So, it cannot be said that in the Vedāntist view the eternity of the Veda is dependent on Īśvara.

It is for this reason that the sūtra, अतएव च नित्यत्वम् of the Uttara Mīmāṁsā becomes very appropriate for the establishment of the eternity of the Vedas. In the introduction to his comment on this sūtra, Śaṅkara says : 'Though the eternity of the Vedas has been established on the ground that no independent author is remembered, etc.,' and thus considering that this

1. Indian Antiquary, Vol. L., pp. 171-2.

matter has already been settled in the Pūrva Mīmāṁsā, he indicates that this sūtra is necessary for removing other doubts. This remark of Śaṅkara clearly tells us that there is an intimate connection between the Pūrva and the Uttara Mīmāṁsās and that the Bādarāyaṇa who is mentioned in the औत्पत्तिक sūtra is none other than the author of the Vedānta-Sūtras. There is no dispute that it is only in the औत्पत्तिक sūtra that the lack of evidence of accredited authorship has been put forth as the reason while establishing a permanent connection between words and their meanings, and that the same reason has served to establish the eternity of the Vedas also. Had Śaṅkara not understood that the reason assigned in the औत्पत्तिक sūtra for proving the eternity of the Vedas (viz., the non-recollection of any author) was approved of by his Sūtrakāra (whose name is mentioned in that sūtra), it would not have been possible for him to make the above remark ('though the eternity of the Vedas has been established on the ground that no independent author of them is remembered,') while explaining a sūtra of the Uttara Mīmāṁsā. If any other Bādarāyaṇa had established the eternity of the Vedas by adopting the above reason, Śaṅkara would certainly have not recognised that conclusion as a decisive one. There is no reason why a Vedāntin Bādarāyaṇa should not prove afresh what has already been proved by a Mīmāṁsist Bādarāyaṇa.

Again, it cannot be suggested that the above remark of Śaṅkara has no reference to the औत्पत्तिक sūtra, for the Bhāmatī has removed all possible doubts by saying, —In the Pūrva Mīmāṁsā the eternity of the Vedas has been established; what is the good of establishing it again ?. Therefore, he (Śaṅkara) says, 'svatantrasya, etc.' The position has been made clearer in the Kalpataru : He (Śaṅkara) says, svatantrasya, etc, to avoid a conflict with the śāstra-yonitva sūtra.' This means that the use of the word 'svatantra' denotes that though the name of an author may be recollected, still he has no independent control.

Thus, on a closer scrutiny, we find that there is no difference between the two systems on this most vital point and that the Bādarāyaṇa, whose name is mentioned in the औत्पत्तिक sūtra, is the same person as the author of the Vedānta-Sūtras.

The second argument is that as Śaṅkara has treated the same sūtra of Jaimini as the pūrvapakṣa view to be refuted by him it cannot contain the view of his own Sūtrakāra. Let us see if this argument, too, holds good. We should ascertain in the first place whether the conclusion of Jaimini has at all been treated as the pūrvapakṣa view by Śaṅkara. It is true that Śaṅkara has used the expression, अनपेक्षत्वात्, for strengthening his pūrvapakṣa in his comment on the sūtra, शब्द इति चेन्नातः प्रभवात् प्रत्यक्षानुमानाभ्याम्[1]. The view stated in the pūrvapakṣa is that the ideas of words are of the form of individuals. But, this is not the view of the Mīmāṁsakas; for, the Mīmāṁsakas hold that concepts are general ideas. So, it cannot be said that in the said pūrvapakṣa the Mīmāṁsaka view has been stated. So, in order to show that there is no conflict with the

1. Vedānta-Sūtra 1. iii. 28.

औत्पत्तिक sūtra Saṅkara states that words convey general conceptions and not conceptions of individuals. It is not a fact that, in the औत्पत्तिक sūtra, the view that words express individual representations is supported by using the expression अनपेक्षत्वात्. Śaṅkara simply concludes that the said pūrvapakṣa cannot arise because both Jaimini and Bādarāyaṇa are of the opinion that concepts of words are general representations. So, this furnishes an additional ground for supposing that in the opinion of Śaṅkara the Bādarāyaṇa of the औत्पत्तिक sūtra is the same as the author of the Vedānta-Sūtras. Mr. Shastri has failed to notice that the pūrvapakṣa is not constructed in accordance with any conclusion of the Mīmāṁsakas but in accordance with a view opposed to the conclusion of the औत्पत्तिक sūtra. Probably the word अनपेक्षत्वात् in the pūrvapakṣa of Śaṅkara has led Mr. Shastri to suppose that the fifth sūtra forms the basis of the pūrvapakṣa.

Following Upavarṣa, Śabara and Saṅkara we have all along supposed that the word बादरायणस्य in the fifth sūtra is connected with the word अव्यतिरेक; but, the position will not be altered even if we connect it with अनपेक्षत्वात् and औत्पत्तिक.

Thus, we see that the arguments advanced by Mr. Shastri are not strong enough to convince us that the Bādarāyaṇa of the fifth sūtra is not the same person as the author of the Vedānta-Sūtras.

In the devatādhikaraṇa[1] of the Pūrva Mīmāṁsā, Śabara and others have propounded the theory of the

---

1. Jaimini-Sūtra IX. i. 4.

uon-existence of physical forms of gods not on the basis of any sūtra of Jaimini but on that of the Uttara Mīmāṁsā. The sūtra[1] चोदना पुनरारम्भः of Jaimini is interpreted as meaning that there is an 'apūrva' which is quite independent of the favour of gods. The comprehensive word, ārambha, does not necessarily mean that the favour of gods is excluded; and, we cannot obtain an interpretation of the sūtra unless we refer to the corresponding sūtras[2] of the Uttara Mīmāṁsā. Similarly, other instances may be cited to show that some sūtras of the Pūrva Mīmāṁsā clearly indicate a previous existence of the sūtra of the Uttara Mīmāṁsā. The doctrines of the want of origin of the Veda etc., are no doubt more fully dealt with in the Pūrva Mīmāṁsā; but, the discussions of these matters are also found in the Uttara Mīmāṁsā, which can stand by themselves without any reference to the Pūrva Mīmāṁsā. That the Uttara Mīmāṁsā is a self-contained system has been graphically shewn by Appyaya Dīkṣita in his famous commentary, Parimala. 'Here (in the Uttara Mīmāṁsā) also the authoritativeness of the Vedic texts forms the subject-matter of the sūtras as in the Pūrva Mīmāṁsā. The sūtra अतएव च नित्यत्वम्[3] establishes the authoritativeness of the Vedic texts. The sūtra नानाशब्दादिभेदात्[4], deals with difference of words, etc. The sūtras शब्दादेव प्रमितः[5], आकाशस्तल्लिङ्गात्[6], तथा चैकवाक्यतोपबन्धात्[7], प्रकरणात्[8], श्रुत्यादिबलीयस्त्वाच्च न

---

1. Jaimini-Sūtra II. i. 5.
2. Vedānta-Sūtra III. ii. 40.
3. op. cit. I. iii. 29.
4. op. cit. III. iii. 58.
5. op. cit. I. iii. 24.
6. op. cit. I. i. 22.
7. op. cit. III. iv. 24.
8. op. cit. I. iii. 6.

भेदः[1], etc., ascertain the principles of śruti (direct texts), liṅga (sense), etc., and their respective value. The sūtras, विपर्ययेण तु क्रमः[2], etc., show how to determine the order of various things. The sūtra अतिदेशाच्च[3] establishes the rule of transference. So, all the things dealt with in the Pūrva Mīmāṁsā are found in the Uttara-Mīmāṁsā-Sūtras. Our revered preceptor, Vācaspati Miśra, has said no doubt that the principles of śruti, liṅga, etc., have been determined in the Pūrva Mīmāṁsā. But, he has nowhere said that it (i.e., the Uttara Mīmāṁsā) depends upon the Pūrva Mīmāṃsā[4]. It cannot be said that in the cases mentioned above the Pūrva-Mīmāṁsā-Sūtras are stated in brief and that the corresponding Uttara-Mīmāṁsā-Sūtras serve as their explanations; for, the sūtras of Jaimini are not only brief but they are so incomplete also that without a reference to the Uttara-Mīmāṁsā-Sūtras it is not possible to make out the correct meanings from them.

Again, the Pūrva Mīmāṁsā imitates the style of the Uttara Mīmāṁsā. Prof. Max Müller seems to be of the same opinion. 'While Bādarāyaṇa begins his Sūtras with 'Athā'to Brahmajijñāsā.......Jaimini apparently in imitation of it begins with 'Athā'to Dharmajijñāsā...'[5]. Hence, it may be presumed that the Uttara-Mīmāṁsā-Sūtras were the first to come into existence.

---

1. Vedānta-Sūtra III. iii. 49.
2. op. cit. II. iii. 14.
3. op. cit. III. iii. 46.
4. Parimala, Nirnayasagar ed. p. 64.
5. Six systems of Indian Philosophy. p. 261.

Now, it may be asked whether the two persons, named Bādarāyaṇa and Jaimini, actually composed these sūtras. Let us first quote what Prof. Max Müller has said on this point : 'Bādarāyaṇa is likewise acquainted with the atheistical doctrines of Kapila and the atomistic theories of Kaṇāda and tries to refute them. But, in India this is far from proving the later date of Bādarāyaṇa. We must learn to look on Bādarāyaṇa, Jaimini, Kapila and similar names as simply eponymous heroes of different philosophies; so, at whatever time these systems were reduced to the form of sūtras, certain opinions could be called by their names. Colebrooke states on the authority of a scholiast of Manu and Yājñavalkya that the instructions of a teacher were often reduced to writing by his pupils, and that these would account for the fact that the author of a system is often quoted in the third person in his book.'[1]

But, the mere fact that the author is quoted in the third person in his book is not sufficient to prove that the book was not written by the author himself. These sūtras are not written in the style in which books are written in present times. If an author wanted to attach his name to his work, he could not put it at the beginning or at the end of the sūtras; for, nothing could be attached to the sūtras which was not connected with the subject-matter. He could not, on the other hand, omit to mention his name; for, then there would be a misapprehension that the sūtras were of a supperhuman origin. He could not also use the first person as it

1. Six systems of Indian Philosophy, p. 158.

would not denote any particular person. Where the name of the author is given either at the beginning or at the end of a book, there the use of the first person, such as 'my view', 'I hold this', etc., can show who is referred to by the first person; but, where the name of the author is not found at all the use of the first person would be useless. So, the only way left open to the author was to insert his name in the sūtras in connection with some particular theory or view of his own.

Though Prof. Keith says : 'We have no valid reason for assuming that the sūtras were actually redacted by Jaimini and Bādarāyaṇa themselves, and unless this is established the argument for contemporaneity is invalid'[1] still we do not think that there is any harm in assuming that they themselves redacted the sūtras. Somebody must have redacted the sūtras; for, they could not come into existence without an author; and our task will indeed be much lighter if the reputed author can be proved to be the real author. There is a strong tradition which says that Jaimini and Bādarāyaṇa actually wrote the sūtras. We have never doubted that the Raghuvaṁśa is a work of a Kālidāsa although it is nowhere found that he is the author of the work. Here we have depended only upon traditions. Where no other relationship is not traceable traditional appellations are usually regarded as denoting authorship. In the Pūrva Mīmāṁsā discussions have been made regarding the appellations, Kāṭhaka, Kālāpaka, etc., and Jaimini would certainly have held that

1. Karma-Mimāṁsā p. 5.

Kaṭha and Kalapa were the authors of certain portions of the Vedas, had not the Vedas been regarded to be of divine origin. We ought not to ignore the value of such traditional appellations, as 'Jaimini-Sūtram,' 'Bādarāyaṇa-Sūtram,' etc. unless we find strong reasons against it. We have shewn above that it is reasonable to believe that Bādarāyaṇa and Jaimini were contemporaries and that the latter wrote his sūtras after the former. It is true that the views of the other systems are found in these sūtras; but, that fact alone does not upset our conclusion. We do not propose to hold that the theories of other systems were not in existence before Bādarāyaṇa or Jaimini wrote his sūtras. It will be rather a mistake to imagine that the Mīmāṁsā as a science did not develop before Jaimini. The very name 'sūtra' or 'thread' implies that it was meant to compress a large amount of matter within a short compass so that it might not be a burden on the memory. 'The main object of the Sūtras', says Prof. Macdonell, 'is therefore, to supply a short survey of these scattered details.'[1] Unless a thing had been very large there would have been no necessity for embodying it into sūtras. But, such a growth must have required a great length of time. So, it is very likely that during that time the views of one system should have been discussed in another. It will be out of place here to try to ascertain the order of priority amongst the Sūtrakāras of all the Darśanas. All that we want to assert here is that Bādarāyaṇa and Jaimini were not mythical heroes of their systems but they did

1. History of Sanskrit Literature, Chap. II.

actually write the sūtras which tradition ascribes to them.

Now, if the time of composition of the Uttara-Mīmāṁsā-Sūtras be prior to that of the Pūrva-Mīmāṁsā-Sūtras, the division of the Mīmāṁsā into a first part and a second part, as has been made in the Seśvara Mīmāṁsā, will not be tenable. It will be preposterous to maintain that what was written subsequently should form the first part. So, the words 'pūrva' and 'uttara' were not used with reference to chronology.

What should then be the principle of the division? If, instead of thinking that the Pūrva Mīmāṁsā and the Uttara-Mīmāṁsā are two parts of the same system having the same aim we assume that they are independent systems having different aims, we shall have an easy answer to the question. The aim of the Pūrva Mīmāṁsā is the purification of the mind of a man by means of various rituals. Until a man's mind is sufficiently purified he cannot understand the frailty of worldly matters; and, so, he is not fit to study the Uttara Mīmāṁsā which preaches that Brahman is the only reality and that the ultimate goal of human life should be the absorption of the individual soul in Brahman. Thus, we find that there are two distinct aims, one of which is only a prelude to the other. That system which deals with the former is the Pūrva Mīmāṁsā and that which deals with the latter is the Uttara-Mīmāṁsā. Prof. Keith supports this view when he says: 'The Mīmāṁsā is prior to the Vedānta, because it deals with the sacred rites, the knowledge of which in the view of one school of the Vedānta is an indispensable preliminary to the knowledge of the absolute.'[1] This statement of Prof. Keith, however, seems to be a representation of the view of the Viśiṣṭādvaita system[2] and not of Saṅkara; for, he himself writes later: 'Though Śaṅkara declines to accept this view and insists instead on the diverse character of the two disciplines which renders it impossible to treat the former as the normal or necessary prelude to the the latter'.[3] Śaṅkara has held, no doubt, that it is possible for a man who has read the Vedānta to have a desire for knowing Brahman even without desiring to know what dharma is[4]. What Śaṅkara means is that in this life some 'persons may have Brahma-jijñāsā without dharma-jijñāsā; but, that it is possible for those persons only who performed in their previous lives all the necessary duties prescribed in the Pūrva Mīmāṁsā and possess in this life, as a consequence of such performances, a sufficient amount of restraint of senses, etc., either in their childhood or during their student-life. It is for such persons only that the following injunctions of the Śruti, 'Brahmacaryād eva pravrajet,' 'Yad ahar eva vrajet tad ahar eva pravrajet,' etc., are intended. But, at any rate this is not the prelude to Brahma-jijñāsā in the case of all ordinary persons. The Bhāmatī clearly states that this is the implication of Śaṅkara.[5] We do

1. Keith, Karma-Mimāṁsā, p. 6.
2. धर्मविबोधानन्तर्यमथशब्दार्थः—Śaṅkara-Bhāṣya, p. 5.
3. Keith, Karma-Mīmāṁsā, p. 6.
4. न, धर्मजिज्ञासायाः प्रागप्यधीतवेदान्तस्य ब्रह्मजिज्ञासोपपत्तेः— Śaṅkara-Bhāṣyā, pp. 68.

5. एवं चाननुष्ठितकर्मापि प्राग्भवीयकर्मवशाद् यो विशुद्धसत्त्वः, संसारासारतादर्शनेन निष्पन्नवैराग्यः, कृतं तस्य कर्मानुष्ठानेन वैराग्योत्पादोपयोगिना प्राग्भवीयकर्मानुष्ठानेनैव तत्सिद्धेः । Bhāmatī, p. 63.

not know on what authority Prof. Keith makes the remark quoted above. It is clear that Śaṅkara, instead of taking an exception to the view, supports it fully.

As we see that according to these eminent authorities the aim of the Pūrva Mīmāṁsā is a necessary prelude to the object of the Uttara Mīmāṁsā, we may safely conclude that the epithets, 'pūrva' and 'uttara', have been used only with reference to different aims and to nothing else.

KUMĀRILA AND PRABHAKARA

Of the two principal schools of the Pūrva Mīmāṁsā the Bhāṭṭa school has all along attracted greater attention than the Prābhākara school. The study of the works of the Prābhākara school has been neglected for a long time past. All the knowledge that our old Sanskrit scholars had of the tenets of this school was derived solely from the stray references found in the works of other systems. One of the earliest works of this school that has been recently published is Śālikanātha's Prakaraṇa-pañcikā. This work epitomises many characteristic tenets of the Prābhākara school. Dr. Ganganath Jha has written a very learned thesis in which he has presented in a lucid form the main principles of the Prābhākara school as they have been dealt with in the Prakaraṇa-pañcikā. He has also given for the first time, much valuable information regarding the Bṛhatī of Prabhākara which is a commentary on Śabara's Bhāṣya.

Dr. Jha has tried to show that though there are traditional stories which tell us that Prabhākara was a pupil of Kumārila, there is no internal evidence proving this relationship. He has suggested that Prabhākara's works belong to a period earlier than that of Kumārila. Dr. Keith has, in his book, the Karmamīmāṁsā, repeated the opinion of Dr. Jha and has gone even a step further in asserting that Śālikanātha also belonged to the ante-Kumārila period.

In the Second Oriental Conference[1] Prof. Kuppuswami Śāstri read a paper in which he thoroughly discussed the above points. He has attempted to support the tradition on historically acceptable grounds. To understand the matter properly it will be necessary for us to see from what data Dr. Jha has drawn his conclusions and whether the grounds given by Prof. Śāstrī are sufficient for a refutation of that conclusion. The following is an extract from the book of Dr. Jha mentioned above.

'As regards the time and place where Prabhākara rose we have not been able to obtain any information except certain traditional stories current among Pundits. According to these Prabhākara along with Maṇḍana Miśra was a pupil of Kumārila. From the very beginning of his studies, he evinced great independence of thought and opinion, and many a story is told in exemplification of his independent spirit......................... The teacher was so pleased at the ingenuity of his pupil that he, thereupon, conferred upon him the title of 'Guru' or 'Teacher'. That the tradition bearing upon the relation of Prabhākara to Kumārila is not a mere lip-story is proved by the following extract from

1. Held at Calcutta in 1922.

an old ms. of the Sarva-siddhānta-rahasya by Śeṣa commented upon by his son, Govinda, a pupil of the great Madhusūdana :—

अस्यां सूत्रं जैमिनीयं शाबरं भाष्यमस्य तु ।
मीमांसावार्त्तिकं भाट्टं भट्टाचार्यकृतं हि तत् ॥
तच्छिष्योऽप्यल्पभेदेन शाबरस्य मतान्तरम् ।
प्रभाकरगुरुश्चक्रे तद्धि प्राभाकरं मतम् ॥

तस्य भाष्यवार्त्तिककर्तुर्भट्टाचार्यस्य शिष्यः प्रभाकरगुरुर्भट्टमतादुपादानग्राहकग्रहणादिरूपप्रमाणान्तरनियोगशब्दबलवादार्थवादादि-रूपषड्भेदस्वीकारेण शाबरस्य शवरस्वामिकृतस्य भाष्यस्य मतान्तरं प्राभाकरं नाम ग्रन्थभेदं कृतवानित्यर्थः :—

In regard to the relation between Kumārila and Prabhākara as indicated by the above tradition, it may be noted that it is not borne out by the internal evidence available in the writings of these authors :

(A) Prabhākara's Bṛhatī is a 'comment', in the strict sense of the word, upon Śabara's Bhāṣya; it does not in any place differ from the original, which it always tries to support; nor does it attack any opinions of the original; in fact, as a rule it attacks no opinions except those of the avowed pūrvapakṣa. Kumārila, on the other hand, in many places in the Tantra-vārttika, rejects the interpretation of Śabara and offers an entirely different interpretation of his own. If Prabhākara had been an innovator or reformer or improver of the Bhāṭṭa system, he would naturally have taken up every one of these deviations from the Bhāṣya and tried to demolish it with his wonted verve and vigour. As a matter of fact, however, we find that the Bṛhatī takes no notice of any of the new interpreations proposed by Kumārila. This would perhaps indicate that it was Kumārila and not Prabhākara, who was an innovator or reformer. This view is confirmed by the fact that while Prabhākara does not criticise any of the strikingly original interpretations of Kumārila the latter in many places, takes great pains to demolish certain views, a few of which have been noticed by Prabhākara in the Bṛhatī. We append a few of these :—

(a) I. ii. 31. (Tantra-vārttika, Translation p. 54.) Kumārila objects to the question of the adhikaraṇa being put in the form : 'Are mantras meaningless or not ?', the form in which it has been stated in the Bṛhatī. (ms. p. 31 a).

(b) I. iii. 2. (Tantravārttika, Translation p. 31 a). According to Prabhākara (ms. p. 31b) the Vedic texts in corroboration of injunctions found in the Smṛti are to be inferred. This is objected to by Kumārila.

(c) I. iv. 1. As regards the connection of pāda iv with the subject-matter of the whole adhyāya Prabhākara, in agreement with the Bhāṣya, puts forward the question in the form : Are the words, udbhid and the like, expressive of materials or names of sacrifices ?'–this question has bearing upon the authority of dharma (Bṛhatī p. 38 a). This is objected to by Kumārila (Tantravārttika, Trans. p. 373).

(d) I. iv. 1. On the same adhikaraṇa, the Bhāṣya and the Bṛhatī with it, take sūtra 1 as the pūrvapakṣa and sūtra 2 as the siddhānta; while Kumārila takes the two sūtras as embodying two distinct adhikaraṇas and objects to the other interpretation. (Tantravārttika Trans. p. 373).

The only point where we have found Prabhākara combating a view propounded by Kumārila is under IV. i. 2 (Bṛhatī ms, p. 64 b, line 9 et seq)., But, in this connection, also, it is noteworthy that the words in which the view combated is expressed—which are apparently a quotation—are very different from those employed by Kumārila (IV. i. 2). The words of the latter are : क्रत्वर्थे द्रव्यार्जने शरीरनाशात् while those used by Prabhākara are—'क्रत्वर्थत्वे स्वत्वमेव न भवतीति याग एव न संवर्तेत' and this is combated by Prabhākara in the words :

प्रलपितमिदं केनापि अर्जनं स्वत्वं नापादयतीति विप्रतिषिद्धम्

The difference in the words shows that 'kenā'pi' of Prabhākara must refer to some one entirely different from Kumārila... ... ...

(B) In point of style also, the Bṛhatī shows distinct signs of being older than the Tantravārttika...'[1]

Thus, we see that Dr. Jha has adduccd external evidence showing that Prabhākara was a pupil of Kumārila and internal evidence as well from their own works indicating that Prabhākara was anterior to Kumārila. It is clear enough that the internal evidence far outweighs the external. His principal argument is that Kumārila's Vārttika is nowwhere referred to in the Bṛhatī whereas the Bṛhatī is referred to in many places in the Tantravārttika.

---

1. Indian Thought pp. 120-34.

Against this Prof. Kuppswami Śāstrī urges that Śālikanātha who was a direct pupil of Prabhākara, has referred to the Ślokavārttika in several places of his Prakaraṇa-pañcikā, Ṛju-vimalā and Pariśiṣṭa. Hence, he supposes that Prabhākara was not anterior to Kumārila. We quote his own words below :

'Prabhākara, Śālikanātha and Bhavanātha are the three greatest exponents of the Prābhākara school so far definitely known to us. Śālikanātha in the first verse of Nītipatha (Section II of Prakaraṇa-pañcikā) refers to himself as Prabhākara's pupil. In the Prakaraṇa-pañcikā, several quotations from the Ślokavārttika are found. For instance, on pages 5, 114, and 122 of the Benares Sanskrit Series edition of the Prakaraṇa-pañcikā the following verses from the Ślokavārttika are found :—

'अथातो धर्मजिज्ञासासूत्रमाद्यमिदं कृतम् ।' page 4.
'गेहाभावस्तु यःशुद्धः · · · · ' p. 445.
'स्वरूपमात्रं दृष्ट्वापि······' p. 483.

Simiiar quotations from Kumārila Bhaṭṭa's Ślokavārttika are found in Śālikanātha's Ṛju-vimalā and Pariśiṣṭa.... ... ...
Again, in the Tarkapāda of the Ṛjuvimalā, on the first leaf ....
which is found in a crumbling condition, I find the following portion of the avatarikā to the first sentence in the Bṛhatī.

'लोक इत्यादि भाष्यं यत्नगौरवं प्रसज्येतेत्येवं (broken) वार्त्तिककारेण व्याख्यातम् । तत्तु मन्दप्रयोजनमिति मत्वा टीकाकारः प्रयोजनं दर्शयति—लोक इत्यादिभाष्यस्य इत्यादिना ।'

The following further extract also from the same broken leaf is worthy of note :—

'......... त्वादविप्रतिपन्नत्वाच्च अथातःशब्दयोरेवालौकिकार्थाशङ्कानिवृत्तिः......प्रयोजनं ....'

However imperfect the above extracts may be, to my mind it is clear that two inferences could be unmistakably drawn from them. Firstly, Śālikanātha assumes that Prabhākara is refuting the views of the Vārttikakāra with reference to the purpose of the opening sentence of the Bhāṣya. Secondly, Prabhākara interprets the Bhāṣyakāra as re-affirming the view of an earlier commentator, that 'athā'taḥ' should be interpreted as a single significative unit. Though, I agree with Dr. Ganganath Jha in thinking that there might have been more than one Vārttikakāra, and that one of them was Kumārila and the 'Vārttikakāra' quoted frequently by Śālikanātha and Bhavanātha in support of the Prābhākara doctrines must have been different from Kumārila and probably earlier than both Kumārila and Prabhākara, yet I am strongly inclined to think that the Vārttikakāra referred to in the above extract from the Ṛju-vimalā must be Kumārila himself, one important reason being that the above Vārttikakāra is generally found invoked only in support of Prabhākara's view and not for offering refutatory comments.'

Let us now examine the grounds on which the assertion that Śālikanātha was a direct pupil of Prabhākara rests. In the first verse of the second section of the Prakaraṇa-pañcikā we find the passage 'प्रभाकरगुरोः शिष्यैः'. Prof. Kuppuswami Śāstri interprets this as meaning that the author was a pupil of Prabhākara. But, it is evident that the word 'guru' does not mean here a preceptor. Had it meant a preceptor it should have been placed as the first part of the compound as 'गुरु-प्रभाकरस्य', and not as the second part.

It is well-known that गुरु was a title of Prabhākara, and there is little doubt that it has been used here as such. Again, the word गुरु has been used in the singular number and the word शिष्य in the plural. This is simply preposterous. It is too well-known that the plural number denotes dignity, and the names of all revered persons, are, therefore, always used in the plural number. We cannot believe that Śālikanātha was so impertinent that he arrogated all the dignity to himself to the exclusion of his preceptor who was no less a personage than Prabhākara himself. Hence, it is not proper to infer from this passage that Śālikanātha was a direct pupil of Prabhākara. That Śālikanātha flourished at a later time is borne out by evidence gathered from the Prakaraṇa-pañcikā itself. All of us know that in the Prakaraṇa-pañcikā two pūrvapakṣas regarding the injunction for Vedic study have been framed one after another. The first of them runs thus : अन्ये पुनरेवं पूर्वंपक्षयन्ति, अध्यापनविधिप्रयुक्तमध्ययनमध्यापनाङ्गम्. It purports to follow the line indicated by Prabhākara; but, still, it is rejected and another pūrvapakṣa तस्मादनङ्गं तथैव पूर्वंपक्षणीयम् is proposed[1]. There is no doubt that the passage—प्रयोज्यत्वादनङ्गत्वाच्च संशयः of the Bṛhatī is the root of both of these pūrvapakṣas. From this we can infer that the above passage of the Bṛhatī was different-

1. Prakāraṇa-pañcikā p. 8.

ly understood by different persons, and that Śālika-nātha wants to point out its true purport by correcting the errors committed by the other followers of Prabhākara. It is not probable that such different interpretations took place during the life-time of the author himself or that of his direct pupils. It is more probable that there came a time when the proper study of the works of Prabhākara fell off. At that time people felt a difficulty in ascertaining the true interpretation of Prabhākara's works. The very manner in which the two divergent pūrvapakṣa views have been put forward in the Prakaraṇa-pañcikā, clearly indicates that it was composed at such a time, and unless we assume the existence of such a state of things it will not be possible to explain why such an important passage of the Bṛhatī should be so differently understood and why Śālika-nātha should assert something as the true view of Prabhākara.

The study of the works of Kumārila has all along been continuously carried on and that is certainly one of the reasons for the wide dissemination of his doctrines; on the other hand, the deterioration in the study of the Prābhākara system has been the main cause of the want of its circulation. We have seen that there are traditional stories which tell us that Prabhākara was a pupil of Kumārila; but, at the same time, there are other similar stories from which we learn that it was Kumārila who destroyed the system of Prabhākara. It clearly appears from the tenth verse of the Pratijñā-sūtra that Kumārila had a very bitter feeling against an older system (of Bhartṛmitra and others) which, as Prof. Śāstri says, was identical with the Prābhākara system. That verse runs thus :—

'प्रायेणैव हि मीमांसा लोके लोकायतीकृता ।
तामास्तिकपथे कर्तुमयं यत्नः कृतो मया ॥'

'The Mīmāṁsā has been reduced almost to a heretical system in this world. I make this attempt to revert it to the orthodox line.' In the Nyāyaratnākara this verse has been explained as follows :—

'नित्यकर्मणां फलं नास्तीति बहुसिद्धान्तपरिग्रहेण
मीमांसा भर्तृमित्रादिभिर्लोकायतीकृता'

'Bhartṛmitra and others have reduced the Mīmāṁsā to a heterodox system by adopting many wrong conclusions, such as, 'the compulsory duties bring in no rewards', etc. But, Bhartṛmitra and others obeyed the authorities of the Vedas as much as Kumārila did. So, it is not at all probable that they actually preached heterodox doctrines like the followers of the Cārvāka school. This vilification must have been, therefore, made by Kumārila out of spite against Bhartṛmitra and his followers. This verse plainly indicates that Kumārila tried his best to put down the rival system, and it corroborates the tradition that Kumārila destroyed the Prābhākara system. So, we see that this tradition is not without foundation; and, hence, we cannot easily ignore it though it contradicts the other tradition mentioned before.

It cannot be fairly contended that Kumārila condemned the doctrines of Bhartṛmitra who had been anterior to him and that Prabhākara, a pupil of Kumārila, simply re-established those doctrines, for it shou'd not be believed for a moment that a pupil made it his sole aim to resuscitate those doctrines which had been openly condemned by his preceptor as heretical.

Thus, it appears that owing to the attacks of Kumārila or for some other reasons the system of Prabhākara fell into a desuetude and men like Śālikanātha attempted to revive it at a later period. Owing to the reasons assigned above we are unable to conclude that Śālikanātha was a direct pupil of Prabhākara.

The next point urged by Prof. Kuppuswami Śāstri, is that Śālikanātha has quoted certain passages from the Ślokavārttika. On a closer scrutiny it will be found that this, also, is not maintainable. The learned professor has pointed out three passages as specimens. The first of them is :

'अथातो धर्मजिज्ञासा सूत्रमाद्यमिदं कृतम्'[1]

This verse has been quoted in the Prakaraṇa-pañcikā in the course of stating a certain view of the Bhāṭṭa school. But, it has beeu quoted after invoking a certain 'Vārttikakāra-miśra,' 'the revered Vārttikakāra'. twice; and, the name of Kumārila has not been mentioned in this connection. Hence, there arises a doubt as to whether this Vārttikakāra-miśra and Kumārila are one and the same person.

In an earlier portion of the Prakaraṇa-pañcikā the appellation, 'Vārttikakāra-miśra', occurs; and, there, too, he is referred to in connection with a pūrva-pakṣa

1. Prakaraṇa-pañcikā, p. 5.

which has been framed in accordance with the Bhāṭṭa point of view. This view is found stated in the Nayaviveka of Bhavanātha in the following words :

'परैरेवं चिन्तितम् , अतोऽतिदेशागतार्थवादावगत-
पितृतृप्तिद्वारकं सार्वात्म्यं भाव्यं कल्प्यम्'[1]

'Others (opponents) think that we should imagine a fruit in the shape of omnipotence which is to be achieved by producing the satisfaction of the manes, and which is connected (with the present injunction) by transferring it from the arthavāda of an analogous injunction'. Here, this view is described as the view of the opponents. Now, if we compare this passage with the said portion of the pūrva-pakṣa of the Prakaraṇa-pañcikā we shall find that it is identically the same thing. That portion runs thus :

तदाहुर्वार्त्तिककारमिश्राः—

'अनुषङ्गानुमानाद्यैर्लभ्यन्तेऽन्येऽतिदेशतः' इति ते अर्थवादा अर्थभावनायां फलं कल्पयन्ति[2] ।

'On this point the revered Vārttikakāra says : 'other arthavādas are obtained by transference through association or inference and those arthavādas supply fruits for the ārthī-bhāvanā'.

So, there is not a shadow of doubt that this 'revered Vārttikakāra' is an opponent of the Prābhākaras. Though this revered Vārttikakāra has been invoked in the Prakaraṇa-pañcikā for supporting the Prābhākara view relating to 'arthāpatti' as a means of proof, still it

1. Nayaviveka, p. 8.
2. Prakaraṇa-pañcika. p. 3.

cannot be said that he is a friend of the Prābhākaras, inasmuch as Kumārila himself holds the same opinion on that point. So, it cannot he maintained that the above Vārttikakāra is generally fourd invoked only in support of Prabhākara's view; and, it seems that the above Vārttikakāra and Kumārila are one and the same person.

But, the verse, 'अनुषङ्गानुमानाद्यैः............', which has been quoted above from the Prakaraṇa-pañcikā does not occur in the Kumārila-Vārttika at all. This fact, along with the other, viz., that Kumārila's name is not specifically mentioned in any of the above cases, can lead to the only conclusion that there was another Vārttikakāra, an earlier originator of the Bhāṭṭa school, from whose works both Kumārila and Śālikanātha have quoted passages. The verse, 'अयातो धर्मजिज्ञासा-सूत्रमाद्यमिदं कृतम्' is most likely a verse of this kind.

The second verse, 'गेहाभावस्तु यः शुद्धः'[1] which is pointed out by Prof. Kuppuswamī Śāstri has also been quoted in the Prakaraṇa-pañcikā after invoking the Vārttikakāra-miśra and not Kumārila. Hence, this verse, too, may be regarded as a composition of that Vārttikakāra and not of Kumārila.

The third verse pointed out by Prof. Śāstri is: 'स्वरूपमात्रं दृष्ट्वा तु'.[2] To this verse the appellation, Vārttikakāra-miśra, is not attached. But, the reading differs palpably from the reading of the Ślokavārttika. In the Prakaraṇa-pañcikā it runs thus :

---

1. Prakaraṇa-pañcikā p. 114.
2. Op. cit. p. 122.

'स्वरूपमात्रं दृष्टं हि वेश्माद्यर्थं स्मरन् पुनः। तत्रान्येनास्तितां पृष्टस्तदेव प्रतिपद्यते ॥'

While in the Ślokavārttika the reading is :

'स्वरूपमात्रं दृष्ट्वापि पश्चात् किञ्चित् स्मरन्नपि। तत्रान्यैर्नास्तितां पृष्टस्तदेव प्रतिपद्यते ।'

The interpretation given in the Prakaraṇa-pañcikā is also different from that given in the Nyāya-ratnākara. In the Prakaraṇa-pañcikā it is introduced to prove that 'anupalabdhi' is not an independent means of proof whereas in the Ślokavārttika it is put forward for establishing the reverse of it. So, it is evident that both the readings have all along been recognised as correct readings and neither of them can be rejected as an erroneous one. How can we say, then, that Śālikanātha has quoted it from Kumārila ? This fact not only negatives the conclusion that Śālikanātha has borrowed verses from Kumārila; but, it also goes to support the other conclusion that both of them have borrowed from some other original sources. They have quoted some verses, word for word; while, in others they have themselves made changes as they thought fit. The readings of the first two verses, therefore, agree exactly with each other, whereas the readings of the third one do not so agree.

The next point urged by Prof. Śāstri is that the Vārttikakāra referred to in the 'avatārikā' to the first sentence of the Bṛhatī in the Ṛjuvimalā of Śālikanātha, is Kumārila himself. Here, Prabhākara is represented as refuting the view of the Vārttikakāra. But, we are to determine whether the particular view that is refuted is actually the view of Kumārila. The interpretation of the expression 'athātaḥ' is here the subject for discussion. In the explanation of the sūtras made by Bhavadāsa and other Vṛttikāras, this expression was treated as a single technical expression. But, all commentators and even Kumārila himself have rejected that interpretation. The following verse of the Ślokavārttika shows that Kumārila has treated this case as one of 'parisaṁkhyā':

'मध्यमे चातिदौर्जन्यात् परिसंख्यैव युज्यते ।'[1]

So, there cannot be any doubt, whatsoever, that Kumārila has not ascribed any technical meaning to the expression. Why should, then, the interpretation of Kumārila be condemned as मन्दप्रयोजन ? If we scrutinise the following passage of the Nayaviveka in which the very same matter has been discussed, we shall be convinced that Kumārila is not the person referred to there. It runs thus :

'परमते लोक इत्यादिभाष्यस्य षडर्थानुक्त्वा दशपक्षी चापरा उक्ता तथाप्यथशब्ददूषणार्थमौचित्यानुभाषणपरत्वमेव स्वीकृतम् ॥'

'The opponents have first stated the six interpretations of the passage, लोक···etc., of the Bhāṣya, and then ten other alternatives......' But, in the Vārttika we do not find the ten other alternatives.

No attempt has been made in the Bṛhatī to support the view of the Vṛttikāra by holding that the expression, 'athātaḥ' is a single word. The Bhāṣya has plainly treated it as consisting of two words, and the Bṛhatī and other commentaries have followed the Bhāṣya in this respect. It is for this reason that the ordinary mean-

1. Pratijñā-Sūtra, verse 47.

ing of the expression has been adopted in the Nayaviveka :

'लौकिकार्थं पदद्वयमिति शास्त्रारम्भः प्रतिज्ञासूत्रम्'[1]

'As the two words have an ordinary sense the Pratijñā-sūtra forms the beginning of the Śāstra.' It is well-known that Bhavadāsa did not attribute any ordinary meaning because he treated the two words as forming one single unit. He is referred to in the Ślokavārttika in this connection :

'वृत्त्यन्तरेषु केषाञ्चिल्लौकिकार्थव्यतिक्रमः'[2]

'In the Vṛttis of some others the ordinary meaning has been given up.' Thus, we see that the Ślokavārttika, the Bṛhatī and the Nayaviveka agree in their conclusion that the expression 'athātaḥ' does not possess any extraordinary meaning. Thus, it is not possible to assume that the word, vārttikakāreṇa, used in the beginning of the Ṛjuvimalā designates Kumārila.

Prof. Kuppuswami Śāstri has spoken of other quotations from the Ślokavārttika which he has found in the Ṛjuvimalā and the Pariśiṣṭha. But, as he has not exhibited them, we are unable to examine them and consequently cannot come to any definite conclusion regarding them. But, until those quotations are shown and judged it can hardly be presumed only on the grounds adduced above that the Vārttikakāra-miśra of the Prakaraṇa-pañcikā is Kumārila. Hence, we are unable to endorse the opinion of Prof. Sāstri : I

1. Nayaviveka, p. 8.
2. Pratijñā-sūtra, verse 33.

am strongly inclined to think that the Vārttikakāra referred to in the above extract from the Ṛjuvimalā must be Kumārila himself, etc.'

Prof. Śāstri next urges that Prabhākara was a contemporary of Kumārila. He says : 'Śālikanātha, who describes himself as Prabhākara's pupil, refers to a Maṇḍana Miśra in his Prakaraṇa-pañcikā, p. 178 in which a well-known verse from Maṇḍana's Vidhiviveka is quoted : 'पुसां नेष्टाऽभ्युपायत्वात्'. Maṇḍana is generally believed to be one of the pupils of Kumārila Bhaṭṭa. Maṇḍana refers to Prabhākara and the Bṛhatī in the Vidhiviveka (already printed) and in the Brahmasiddhi of which my edition is under preparation) in several places with the animus generally characteristic of a contemporaneous opponent.' By analysing this statement we obtain the following facts : Maṇḍana is a pupil of Kumārila, Śālikanātha is a pupil of Prabhākara, Maṇḍana treats Prabhākara in a manner that befits a contemporary and Śālikanātha quotes passages from Maṇḍana's Vidhiviveka. From these facts Prof. Śāstri intends to draw the conclusion that Prabhākara was a contemporary of Kumārila.

But, we have shown above that Śālikanātha was not a pupil of Prabhākara. As regards the assertion that Maṇḍana was a pupil of Kumārila, there is no evidence excepting a popular belief. Even if this belief be regarded as true, still it is not conclusively proved that Prabhākara was contemporaneous with or posterior to Kumārila; but, it may rather prove that Prabhākara was anterior to Kumārila. Then, it is not also proper to conclude that Prabhākara was Maṇḍana's contemporary merely from the fact that Maṇḍana attacked the views of Prabhākara with an animus characteristic of a contemporaneous opponent, as it is nothing unusual in our country for the followers of one school to atack the doctrines of the founder of a rival school who flourished long ago with great animus. So, the only thing that remains for our consideration is the statement that Śālikanātha has quoted a passage from Maṇḍana's Vidhiviveka. But, we shall not practically gain much by discussing this point; for, even if it is found to be correct, we shall only learn that Śālikanātha was posterior to Maṇḍana Miśra and nothing more.

Last of all, Prof. Śāstri comes to the central point of the subject of his discussion, viz., that Prabhākara was a pupil of Kumārila. He cites a verse which has been traditionally handed down, in which the name of Prabhākara is placed between two other names which Prof. Śāstri supposes to be the names of two pupils of of Kumārila; and, hence, he concludes that Prabhākara must have been a pupil of Kumārila.

The verse runs thus :

'उम्वेकः कारिकां वेत्ति तन्त्रं वेत्ति प्रभाकरः ।
मण्डनस्तूभयं वेत्ति नोभयं वेत्ति रेवणः ॥'

Prof. Śāstri asserts that both Umveka and Maṇḍana are pupils of Kumārila. We have already discussed the question of relationship between Maṇḍana and Kumārila. Let us now see how Prof. Śāstri makes out that Umveka was a pupil of Kumārila. He finds his strongest evidence in the Sāstradīpikā :

'अत्रोम्वेकभट्टैरिदन्तु वार्त्तिककारीयं दूषणं समर्थनञ्च सर्व-मेवालूनविशीर्णमित्यादिना...............गुरोरप्यवलिप्तस्य कार्याकार्यमजानतः। उत्पथं प्रतिपन्नस्य परित्यागो विधीयते ॥ इत्यन्तेन ग्रन्थेन भाष्यं वार्त्तिकञ्च दूषितम् ।'

The above extract from the commentary of the Śāstradīpikā[1] would appear to leave no alternative except to assume that Umveka Bhaṭṭa was one of the pupils of Kumārila Bhaṭṭa.

But, we do not think that from this extract of the Śāstradīpikā we are justified in concluding that Umveka was a direct pupil of Kumārila. In the very beginning of the commentary on the Śāstradīpikā we find this passage :

'उक्तञ्च उम्वेकेन, ग्रन्थारम्भेऽभिमतदेवतानमस्कारं करोति वार्त्तिककारः' ।

which contains a quotation from some work of Umveka. Here the word, Vārttikakāra, is in the singular number, and without any such epithet as 'ācārya' etc. Had this Vārttikakāra been the preceptor of Umveka he could never have referred to him in such an unceremonious manner. So, this raises a strong doubt as to whether the relationship of preceptor and disciple existed between these two persons. It may be said that the word 'guru' occurs in the other passage 'गुरोरप्यवलिप्तस्य......' quoted above. But, in this passage the word is used in its general sense and is not meant to refer to the preceptor of the author in particular. It simply indicates that Umveka looked up to Kumārila as a highly revered person and nothing more. Besides, it is evident from the remaining

1. Com., Nirnayasagar Press, p. 30.

portion of the passage that Umveka attacks here the views of both Kumārila and Śabara. So, the word 'guru' must necessarily refer to both of them and not to Kumārila alone. But, Prof. Śāstri would never admit that Umveka was a pupil of Śabara also. Thus, on the grounds stated above it is not possible to conclude that Umveka was a pupil of Kumārila. There is, then, no satisfactory evidence to show that Maṇḍana and Umveka were direct pupils of Kumārila. Consequently, the argument of Prof, Śāstri, that Prabhākara, hemmed in as he is found between the two pupils of Kumārila, would appear to be also one of Kumārila's pupils, loses all force. So, from this verse, उम्वेक: etc. alone we are not justified in concluding that Prabhākara was a pupil of Kumārila.

With reference to the expression 'apasiddhānta' found in the passage, प्रायेण etc., of the Ślokavārttikā quoted above, Prof. Śastri has observed : 'It is noteworthy here that the apasiddhānta referred to in this extract is widely known to the world of Indian Philosophers as one of the distinctive tenets of the Prābhākara school. If, Bhartṛmitra, and not Prabhākara, is associated with this tenet as its exponent as presupposed by Kumārila, one is tempted to fancy that perhaps Prabhākara's relation to Bhartṛmitra was similar to Śaṅkara's relation to Gauḍapāda'. We do not understand exactly what Prof. Śāstri seeks to establish here. If the relation of Prabhākara to Bhartṛmitra be the same as that of Śaṅkara to Gauḍapāda, then Prabhākara must be regarded as a direct pupil of Bhartṛmitra. How can we then say, again, that Prabhākara was a direct pupil of Kumārila ? So, his argument affects the very tradition which he wants to maintain. But, if he regards Bhartṛmitra as the rival founder of the Prābhākara school of which Prabhākara was a later exponent, still he cannot establish that Prabhākara was a pupil of Kumārila; for, we do not know exactly whether he flourished before or at the time of Kumārila.

Thus, on a consideration of all the above points we find that the grounds stated by Prof. Śāstri do not warrant us in drawing any conclusion regarding the relationship between Kumārila and Prabhākara; and, that on the other hand, there is strong evidence, both internal and external, supporting the suggestion made by Dr. Jha, viz., that Prabhākara was anterior to Kumārila.

CHAPTER TWO

PRAMĀ AND PRAMĀṆA

Cognitions are divided into two classes :—(1) pramā or valid cognition, and (2) apramā or invalid cognition. The Bhāṭṭas define valid cognition as that 'which being free from discrepancies apprehends things not already apprehended'. There is practically not much difference between this definition of the Bhāṭṭas and the corresponding definition of the Prābhākaras. But. Dr. Jha is of opinion that the Bhāṭṭas do not accept the definition given by the Prābhākaras and that the definition given by the former is subversive of the 'svataḥ-prāmāṇya' or self-validity of cognition, which forms the very keynote of Mīmāṁsā'.

Dr. Jha derives the Prābhākara definition of pramā from the following verse of the Prakaraṇa-pañcikā :

'प्रमाणमनुभूतिः, सा स्मृतेरन्या न सा स्मृतिः।
न प्रमाणं स्मृतिः पूर्वप्रतिपत्तिव्यपेक्षणात् ॥'

He explains this verse thus :—'That is to say, valid cognition is apprehension, it is totally different from remembrance. which is not valid, inasmuch as it stands in need of a previous cognition, being as it is, a cognition, produced only by the impressions left by a previous cognition.........Thus, remembrance cannot be regarded as valid, because it bears upon its object not directly. but only indirectly through the agency of previous cognitions of that object.'

Here, we notice that remembrance is not regarded as valid cognition, and why? Because, it stands in need of a previous cognition. Thus, according to the author of the Prakaraṇa-pañcikā, the need of a previous apprehension is the cause of the invalidity of remembrance. By this statement of the Prakaraṇa-pañcikā, it is cleerly implied that previous non-apprehension of the object is a criterion of validity.

So, we see that the remark, that valid cognition is but apprehension, pure and simple, does not tally with the view of the Prakaraṇa-pañcikā. Had it been the intention of the author of the Prakaraṇa-pañcikā to define valid cognition as mere apprehension without attaching to it any extraneous condition, such as previous non-apprehension, he would certainly have denied the validity of remembrance on the simple ground that it is not an apprehension; and, he would never have felt the necessity of assigning any other reason.

There is no doubt, therefore, that the condition of not being apprehended before is accepted by both the schools. The only difference between the views of the two schools is that while the Bhāṭṭas impose two conditions, viz., the absence of discrepancies and the previous non-apprehension of the object, the Prābhākaras impose only the latter. That remembrance is no valid cognition is admitted by both the schools. But, there is a difference of opinion regarding such a wrong cognition as that of silver in a conch-shell. The Bhāṭṭas hold that the cognition, viz., 'this is silver', is only one cognition; but, according to the Prābhākaras, there are two cognitions involved in it, of which, one is an apprehension and the other is a remembrance. Dr. Jha has explained this very lucidly, and it is worth while to quote him here: 'The judgement or idea resulting from the cognition, 'this is silver' when referring to the shell, contains not one, but two cognitions, one pertaining to 'silver' and the other to 'this'; and of these two, the idea of 'silver' is mere remembrance; and, as such, not being 'apprehension', it cannot be regarded as valid; the other factor in the idea, i.e., the idea of 'this', is of the nature of apprehension; and, as such, must be regarded as valid. Thus, we find that the wrongness of the judgment 'this is silver' lies in the idea of silver which is remembrance; and, this also is regarded as wrong, simply because it is not found to agree with the real state of things when the agent proceeds to act up to the judgment and picks up the piece. Even those[1] who regard the judgment, 'this is silver', as containing a single idea and as wrong, base the wrongness upon the fact of the judgment being one that is found to be subsequently sublated and not upon anything in the nature of the cognition itself. But, these people also cannot regard as wrong that factor of the judgment which pertains to 'this', as the notion of 'this' is not found to be sublated being retained in the sublating judgment also, which latter is in the form—'this is not silver but shell'[2].

The next question is whether the introduction of the two qualifications would disturb the svataḥ-prāmāṇya of cognitions or not. On this point Dr. Jha

1. The Bhāṭṭas.
2. Indian Thought Vol. II. p. 140.

says : 'If the validity of cognitions depends not upon its own nature, but upon such extraneous circuumstaness as the absence of discrepancies and the previous non-apprehension of the object, then where would be its svataḥ-prāmāṇya or self-validity ?'[1]

It is true that errors, remembrances, apprehensions and other instances of cognition are all valid as cognitions. Even if a cognition is found not to agree with the real state of things, the cognition as cognition cannot but be regarded as valid. But, still, for practical purposes, cognitions are divided into valid and invalid cognitions. If a cognition satisfies such conditions as the absence of discrepancies, or a previous non-apprehension of the object, it is regarded as a valid cognition; otherwise, it is regarded as invalid, in spite of the fact that it is valid as a cognition. We have seen above that the invalidity of remembrance is due to the fact that it depends upon a previous apprehension and not to the fact that the very nature of cognitton is wanting there.

Thus, we see that the expression, 'validity of cognition', is used in two senses. A cognition is valid *per se*, and a cognition is valid which stands the tests mentioned above; or, in other words, there is a validity which is due to an internal cause and there is another validity which depends upon external causes also.

In the Nyāya-ratnāvalī the external causes have been specifically described.[2] It is stated there that the

1. Indian Thought Vol. II. p. 142.
2. Nyaya-ratnāvalī, p. 123.

external causes which make a cognition valid are of two kinds : absence of discrepancies and want of previous apprehension of the object, of which the first is common to remembrance and apprehension and the second is found only in the case of apprehension. In the Vedānta-paribhāṣā, too, it is stated that the validity which depends upon the two factors—absence of discrepancies and previous non-apprehension, does not exist in remembrance; but, that validity which depends upon the absence of discrapencies only is common to remembrance also. On a consideration of these statements we find that three kinds of validity are recognised. The first depends upon absence of discrepancies, and previous non-apprehension, and exists in direct apprehension; the second depends upon absence of discrepancies only and exists both in remembrance and in apprehension; and, the third is inherent in the nature of cognition; and, so, it is present in all kinds of cognition—error, remembrance and apprehension. The first two are known as 'paratogrāhya pramātva', i.e., validity due to extraneous causes, and the third one is called 'svatogrāhya pramātva', i.e., validity due to cognition itself. That Kumārila has recognised this distinction appears from the following passage —

तस्माद् बोधात्मकत्वेन प्राप्ता बुद्धेः प्रमाणता ।
अर्थान्यथात्वहेतूत्थदोषज्ञानादपोद्यते ॥[1]

'The validity of cognition, therefore, lies in its very nature; it is set aside when it is found to be vitiated on account of disagreement with the real state of things'. Here, Kumārila has very briefly spoken of the

1. Ślokavārttika Sū. II, 53.

two kinds of validity. His followers, Pārthasārathi Miśra[1] and other later writers, have, however, put forward the definition of valid cognition as that which, being free from discrepancies, apprehends things not already apprehended. But, they have simply defined the paratogrāhya-pramātva. They have not, as Dr. Jha supposes, 'missed the very point of the dictum of the svataḥ-prāmāṇya of cognitions'; but, they have not clearly drawn a distinction between svatogrāhya-pramātva and paratogrāhya-pramātva. There is no evidence to show that they have denied the self-validity of cognitions, save that they have mentioned the other kind of validity. The mere mention of the parato-grāhya-pramātva, however, does not imply the denial of the svatogrāhya-pramātva, because the former pre-supposes the latter and does not exclude it. As Kumārila himself has definitely accepted the svatogrāhya-prāmāṇya of cognitions, the later text-writers have only taken it for granted. Besides, the svatogrāhya-pramā-tva exists in all cognitions, whereas the paratogrāhya-pramātva exists only in some of them. So, whenever the validity of a cognition is questioned, it is the paratogrāhya-pramātva that is invariably taken into account. This is also another reason why the later writers of the Bhāṭṭa school have defined this kind of validity only. It is clear from their definition, that it is only the paratogrāhya-pramātva that is meant, though, in fact, they have not used that specific name to designate it. In the Laghu-candrikā this parato-grāhya-pramātva has been clearly described as that pramātva which is good for practical purposes :

1. **Śāstradīpikā**, p, 23.

'व्यवहारप्रयोजकं प्रमात्वं, स्वतो ग्राह्यं प्रमात्वञ्च, द्विविधं प्रमात्वं वर्तते ।'[1]

Thus, we see that the expression 'validity' has all along been used in two different senses, between which there is no confusion. There is no reason, therefore, to fear that the svataḥ-prāmāṇya of cognitions will disappear if the validity is made to depend upon extraneous circumstances.

Prabhākara recognises five forms of valid cognition: (1) pratyakṣa (perception); (2) anumāna (inference); (3) upamāna (analogy); (5) śāstra (śabda) and (5) arthāpatti (presumption). Kumārila accepts all these and adds one more, viz, abhāva (non-apprehension). Pratyakṣa proceeds from the direct contact of the sense-organs with the object. Inference is the cognition of an object not in direct contact with the senses, which (cognition) is due to the perception of some other thing, between which and the first object, an invariable connection is known to exist. Upamāna is the cognition of similarity of an object not in contact with the senses to an object which is actually perceived.

Śabda (śāstra) or verbal cognition is the cognition, by virtue of the knowledge of words, of something which is not open to the ordinary means of cognition. Arthāpatti is the presumption of a thing which is necessary for reconciling the apparent incon-

1. Gauḍa-Brahmānandī, Nirṇaya Sāgara Press p. 440.

sistency of any two certain perceptions. Abhāva (non-existence) or anupalabdhi (non-apprehension) is recognised by Kumārila as a separate means of proof. In the case of the judgement, 'there is no jar on the table', the absence of the jar is cognised; but, this cognition is neither perception, nor inference, nor any of the above-mentioned means of proof. Kumārila holds, therefore, that non-apprehension is the only means whereby this absence is cognised. As against this, the Prābhākaras argue that there is nothing which could be cognised by means of non-apprehension; and, therefore, they do not accept anupalabdhi as a distinct means of proof.

It is needless for us to enter here into all the details and differences of views regarding these six pramāṇas. We shall, therefore, briefly mention the necessity of introducing so many pramāṇas into the Mīmāṁsā. The sole business of the Mīmāṁsakas consists in ascertaining dharma i.e., duty. This duty is not a materially existing thing and there is no possibility, therefore, of its ever coming into contact with the sense-organs. Hence, pratyakṣa is of no use here. Similarly, anumāna, upamāna, arthāpatti and anupalabdhi, all of which are dependent more or less upon perception are of no avail in ascertaining dharma. Consequently, the Mīmāṁsakas have accepted the Vedas as the only infallible means of acquiring the knowledge of dharma. Now, if the Vedas be the only means in this respect, why should the other four or five means be at all discussed in the Mīmāṁsā ? To this Śabara Svāmin gives the answer that perception and the other means of proof have been introduced into the Mīmāṁsā not for the purpose of ascertaining dharma through them, but only with a view to satisfying ourselves that dharma cannot be ascertained through them. But, though perception etc. are not directly useful for ascertaining dharma, they are necessary for refuting some of the antagonistic views questioning the authoritativeness of the Vedas and for settling various questions in connection with dharma.

The Saugatas have denied the existence of external entities. They hold that there is no actual existence of external objects as apart from cognitions and that the outside world is nothing but śūnya. This view is clearly in opposition to that of the Śruti. If there be no real existence of paradise, etc., why should the Śruti enjoin sacrifices ? Hence, it is necessary to conclude that the external world does actually exist and that a correct knowledge of it can be derived by perception. It is evident, therefore, that the recognition of perception as a means of proof is not out of place in the Mīmāṁsā. This fact is put very concisely in the following verse of the Ślokavārttika :

इति वहिर्विषयप्रतिपादनात् तदभावकृता मतिसंवृतिः ।
उभयतत्त्वविदां परमार्थतः क्षममिदं धुरि धर्मविचारणे ॥[1]

The false notion that was created by (preaching the theory of) the non-existence of external things is thus (removed) by propounding that they are existent. This (Mīmāṁsā-Śāstra) is able to help those

1. Śūnyavāda, 264.

who believe in the truth of both (cognition and external thing) in discussing dharma.

The usefulness of anumāna lies in making various necessary assumptions. We may cite a well-known case by way of illustration. The authority of Smṛti texts is established by assuming that they have had a Vedic-origin. The Smṛti texts are all human compositions; and, so, their authority regarding matters of dharma is challenged. But, as their authors were pre-eminent Vedic scholars, it is assumed that they have been derived from the Vedas.[1]

In the latter half of the Pūrva-Mīmāṁsā, the question of atideśa or transference is discussed in numerous cases. In all those cases, the usefulness of upamāna or analogy is clearly perceived. We cannot decide that the Saurya sacrifice is to be performed after the manner of the Āgneya sacrifice unless we accept analogy as a valid means of proof. Again, the question of substitution is decided only on the ground of analogy.[2] We quote below the verses of the Sloka-vārttika showing the usefulness of upamāna :—

भिन्नानुमानादुपमेयमुक्ता
सौर्यादिवाक्यैरसहापि दृष्टम् ।
सादृश्यतोऽग्न्यादियुतं कथं नो
प्रत्याययेदित्युपयुज्यते नः ॥
प्रतिनिधिरपि चैवं व्रीहिसादृश्ययोगाद्
भवति तदपचारे यत्र नीवारजातौ ।

1. Jaimini-Sūtra, 1. iii. 1.
2. op. cit. VI. iii. 11, 13–15 etc.

तद्‌पि फलमभीष्टं लक्षणस्योपमायाः
प्रकृतिरपि च गौणैर्बोध्यते यत्र चान्यैः ॥
यदि सुसदृशमेतल् लभ्यते तत्र मिथ्या
भवति विसदृशत्वान् मन्दसादृश्ययुक्तम् ।
मतिरपि च तथैव द्रागिवोत्पद्यतेऽस्मि-
न्नितरविषयबोधे सत्यपीत्थञ्च बाधः ॥[1]

'This upamāna is different from anumāna. The sentence containing the words 'Agni, etc', is not connected with the sentences beginning with Saurya, etc., but, still by analogy it transfers its own details. Here, lies the usefulness (of upamāna). Where 'vrīhi' is lost or is not available 'nīvāra' is accepted as a substitute on account of its similarity to 'vrīhi'. Here, also, upamāna serves a distinct purpose. In some cases the similarity is understood through points of similitude which are not strong and in other cases it is clear, the points of similitude being strong. The former, which is not clearly similar, is useless, because of its less similarity, whereas the latter is accepted readily; and, when it is once accepted, the other one is excluded in spite of its being taken into account.'

The usefulness of arthāpatti as a means of proof is thus set forth in the Ślokavārttika :—

'स्मृत्या श्रुतिर्या परिकल्प्यतेऽस्मि-
ल्लिङ्गादिभिर्या विनियोजिका च ।
फलादिभिर्यत् परिपूरणञ्च
सम्बन्धदृक् तत्र न काचिदस्ति ॥"[2]

1. Upamāna-parichheda, 52-54.
2. Arthāpatti-pariccheda, 87.

'In it (the Pūrva-Mīmāṁsā) an original Vedic text is imagined from the existence of a Smṛti text; a text of the Śruti showing the application of a particular thing is imagined on the liṅga-principle, etc., and results etc. are imagined to make injunctions complete, But, in all these cases there is no means of showing these connections (except arthāpatti)'. We have cited the first of these cases under anumāna. Where there is no direct pronouncement of the Śruti showing an application, an injunction is made out by the suggestive power of ideas, etc. In the injunctions for Viśvajit and some other sacrifices no fruits are mentioned but are imagined. All these things are made out by arthāpatti. It may be said that really speaking there is no distinction between anumāna and arthāpatti. Kumārila, in fact, actually draws a distinction between them, yet at the same time it must be admitted that he is never eager to regard arthāpatti as a separate means of proof. The following stanza clearly sets forth his view :

एवंस्वभावाप्यनुमानशब्दं लभेत चेदस्ति यथेप्सितं नः ।[1]

'Such is (arthāpatti); but, if it still comes to be called anumāna, we give our consent.'

The necessity of adopting anupalabdhi as a separate means of proof is explained by Kumārila in the following verse of the Ślokavārttika :—

'कर्माणि सर्वाणि फलैः समस्तैः सर्वं यथावच्च यदङ्गकाण्डैः ।
न सङ्गतानीह परस्परञ्च नाङ्गं तदेतत् प्रभवं क्रतूनाम् ॥'[2]

---

1. Arthāpatti-pariccheda 88.
2. Abhāva-pariccheda 56.

'All the sacrifices do not produce all the results, nor do they possess all the details, nor are they connected with one another......'. Chapters are devoted in the Pūrva-Mīmāṁsā to discussions regarding differentiation, sublation, etc. According to Kumārila, anupalabdhi is the only means of proof by which the fact, that one sacrifice is not identical with or is not a part of another sacrifice, is known. And, it is also implied by him that it is not possible for the followers of the other schools to make such discriminations.

Thus, we conclude that though dharma is not known directly by these means of proof, still they are absolutely necessary for carrying on various discussions raised in this connection.

We have said above that śabda or word has been accepted by the Mīmāṁsakas as the means for ascertaining dharma. Now, śabda may be of two kinds—Vedic and human. In the Lokavedādhikaraṇa it has been shown that there is no actual difference between Vedic and human words. The meanings of words are known from 'vyavahāra'.[1] But, 'vyavahāra' is possible only in the case of human words, and not in the case of Vedic words. So, if we deny the validity of human words altogether, we shall not be able to know the meanings of Vedic words. This importance of human words has been recognised in the beginning of the Ślokavārttika on the Codanā-sūtra. There is only this difference between a Vedic word and a human word—a human word may or may not be valid, whereas a Vedic word

1. By watching the usage of older persons.

is always valid. This has been propounded by Sabara Svāmin in his commentary on the Codanā-sūtra.

In the sūtra of Jaimini mentioned above, the word, 'codanā', occurs; and, hence, it appears that only those sentences in which an action forms the leading element are to be regarded as authoritative. Jamini keeps this in view when he says that arthavāda texts are authoritative in so far as they contain eulogies which create a tendency in the mind of a man to act.[1] The Vedāntins, on the other hand, recognise authority even of such Vedic texts which do not make the action-element prominent but simply describe saguṇa (immanent) Brahman, nirguṇa (transcendental) Brahman, etc., This is opposed to the purport of the sūtra 'Āmnāyasya etc'.[2] of Jaimini. But, it has been pointed out in the Bṛhatī and other works that there is really no such conflict between the sūtras of Jaimini and the Vedānta doctrines. We shall speak more fully of this in the next chapter.

There is a difference ofopinion between the Bhāṭṭas and the Prābhākaras regarding the way in which the validity of words is made out. It is well known that the Prābhākaras have accepted the theory of anvitābhidhānvāda, and the Bhāṭṭas have accepted abhihitānvayavāda. According to the first theory, two powers of words are recognised—one enables us to remember the meanings and the other establishes the connection between the meanings remembered the former itself, being known first, causes the recollection

1. Jaimini-Sūtra I. ii. 7.
2. op. cit. I. ii. 1.

of meanings, whereas the latter gives rise to knowledge of the connection without itself being known. This second power is known technically as the kubja-śakti.

According to abhihitānvayavāda the knowledge of meanings is due to words; but, that knowledge arises neither through recollection nor through apprehension, but through what is technicaliy called abhidhāna (denotation); and, the knowledge of the connection of the meanings is due to the meanings known. The power of making meaning known is inherent in words; but, the power of giving rise to knowledge of the connection lies in the meanings. According to both the theories. the knowledge of the first power is necessary, but that of the second one is not so.

According to anvitābhidhānavāda, there will be no apprehension of the sense of words unless the words be used. If any one utters the word, 'door', only, we must understand some other word, such as 'shut', to make the sense complete; but, according to the other theory, any two ideas which have been known by some pramāṇa or other, may come to be combined according to necessity; and, hence, we can complete the sense by understanding an idea also. The Ślokavārttika goes a step further when it says :—

'पश्यतः श्वेतिमारूपं ह्रेषाशब्दश्च शृण्वतः ।
खुरनिक्षेपशब्दश्च श्वेतोऽश्वो धावतीति धीः ॥'

'A man who sees something white, hears the neighing of a horse and the noise of hoofs; from these he conceives that a white horse is running.' The matter has been fully dlscussed in the Nyāyaratnāvalī.[1]

1. pp. 43-45.

This difference is not, however, of any practical importance so far as the subject-matter of the Mīmāṁsā is concerned. The ninth chapter of the Mīmāṁsā deals with ūha (substitution). If we accept abhihitānvayavāda, we shall be able to understand all necessary things, and no ūha of words will be necessary. Hence, it may be contended that all discussions regarding ūha are useless. To this the answer of the Bhāṭṭas is that in the case of prakṛti (primary,) ceremonies, things are mentioned by words; and, hence, we must repeat the same process in the case of vikṛti (derivative) ceremonies too.

We notice the importance of the difference between these two theories when the value of the Vedānta system comes in for consideration. The anvitābhidhānavāda excludes the Vedānta doctrines from the province of 'karman'. It recognises the authority of such sentences only where an action is the predominating element; and, hence, the Prābhākaras construe the words of an arthavāda text together with those of a vidhi text[1]. According to the other theory, an arthavāda has a complete sense in itself; and, hence, an entire arthavāda text is simply to be combined with its corresponding vidhi text[2]. The abhihitānvayavāda does not ignore the importance of such texts which simply point out an existing thing; and, hence, it does not stand against the authority of the Upaniṣad texts.

Once more we compare the two theories. According to the anvitābhidhāna theory, words are regarded as

1. Nyāyamālā I. ii. 2.
2. Loc. cit.

valid owing to their connection with an action; otherwise, they will not be valid; because, they give rise to the recollection of meanings. And, remembrance, as we have seen, has no validity. According to the other theory, meanings are regarded as valid and not words, no matter whether there be any connection with an action or not. So, the Bhāṣya says that words stop on expressing their respective meanings and that the meanings, being thus known, make up the meaning of the sentence.[1] So, there is an agreement between the two theories as to the point that words convey their respective meanings; but, while one holds that this conveyance is due to remembrance, the other holds that it is due to abhidhāna. But, this conveyance is not verbal cognition. Verbal cognition is the knowledge of the meaning of one word as connected with the meaning of another; according to the first theory, the knowledge is created by virtue of the words themselves, whereas, according to the other, it is created by virtue of the meanings.

It is very strange that Dr. Jha while explaining anvitābhidhānavāda says that no word can be comprehended as having any denotation when taken apart from an injunctive sentence[2], and both Mr. V. S. Apte[3] and Dr. Keith[4] have made similar statements. But, we have shown above that words do convey their meanings independently, but, for the sake of validity, they have to depend upon other words of the sentence.

---

1. Jaimini-Sūtra I. i. 25. 2. Indian Thought Vol. 11. 236.
3. Apte's Sans. Eng. Dictionary. 4. Karma-mīmāṁsā, p. 39.

CHAPTER THREE

I. ĀTMAN

In most of the sacrificial injunctions we find that the performers of sacrifices are entitled to enjoy results (heaven etc.,) that come after their death. Now, when the performer is dead, he cannot enjoy the fruit. But, the statements of the Śruti cannot be false. There must be some such entity which must last even after the destruction of the body. This entity is called Ātman, and has been regarded as something different from buddhi, the sense-organ and the body.[1]

Buddhi is not identical with Ātman—it is an instrument of cognition and not an agent. The same argument holds good in the case of the sense-organ also. In such ordinary expressions as, 'I who saw the book, am touching it now', the notion of only one cogniser is manifest though two sensc-organs are mentioned[2]. But, it is impossible to identify two or more sense-organs whose forms and functions are quite different. It must, therefore, be admitted that there exists some other entity behind them. Again, the body is not Ātman, because the Śruti indicates that Ātman must persist after the dissolution of the body. Besides, the body changes with age—the body of childhood is not the same as that in youth and the body of youth, again, is

1. Ślokavārtika, Ātmavāda, 5, 6, 7.
2. Śāstradīpikā—Indriyātmabhedaprakaraṇam.

much unlike the body of old age.[1] But, in the midst of these changes the self remains the same; otherwise, how could one say, 'I who saw my parents in my childhood, am seeing my grand-children in my old age ?' Again, pleasure etc. cannot be the properties of the body. If the body be cut open, the inside will be found to be of a certain colour, because colour is a property of the body; but, no such thing as pleasure or pain is ever found there.[2] Hence, there must exist some entity which is the basis of pleasure, pain etc., but which is different from the body. Various other arguments of this nature have been advanced in this behalf in other Āstika Darśanas and have been adopted by Kumārila. It is needless to cite all of them here.

Now, it may be of interest to enquire here, whether the Sūtras of Jaimini can furnish anything whereby the existence of an Ātman different from the body, the sense-organ and buddhi, can be established. The author of the Seśvara-Mīmāṁsā-Darśana[3] is of opinion that the sūtra[4] सत्संप्रयोगे पुरुषस्य इन्द्रियाणां बुद्धिजन्म, etc., of Jaimini leads us to conclude that Jaimini himself gives an idea of an Ātman which is different from the body, etc., because the three words पुरुष, इन्द्रिय and बुद्धि are used separately in the sūtra; again, the word 'पुरुषस्य' is in the genitive case which indicates that one belongs to the other, i.e. one is different from the other; and, hence, from this sūtra, we learn that there is no

1. Bhagavadgītā, II. 12.
2. Ślokavārttika, Ātmavāda, 100.
3. Śrī Vedānta-Deśika.
4. Jaimini-Sūtra I. i. 4.

identity (of Ātman) with buddhi. Ātman is known by all means of knowledge to be the basis of buddhi, and the expression बुद्धिजन्य shows that buddhi has a beginning. Hence, the word पुरुष must mean some cogniser who has no beginning. ... ... The definition of perception etc. will be stated in the Nyāya-vistara. That may have only incidentally been referred to here or not'.[1] Thus, according to Śri Vedānta Deśika, the real object of framing this sūtra is to show that Ātman is different from buddhi etc., as also to prove the uselessness of perception as a means of ascertaining 'dharma'. The differentiation of Ātman from buddhi etc., he asserts, follows directly from the sūtra. Now, we cannot accept this position without a careful examination. In the first place, the sūtra does not contain any word denoting the body, as there are words denoting the sense-organs and buddhi. So, it cannot be said that the identity of Ātman with the body is denied here. There are, no doubt, other means of disproving the identity of Ātman with the body, but if other means have to be adopted for this purpose, they can similarly be had recourse to for

---

1. पुरुषस्येति सम्बन्धकथनात् तच्च सूचितम् ।
बुद्धितो व्यतिरिक्तत्वमतएव च सूत्रितम् ॥
तद्धर्मित्वेन सकलैः प्रमाणैरुपलम्भनात् ।
बुद्धेर्जन्मेत्यनेनैव बुद्धेर्जन्मप्रदर्शनात् ॥
अजातः प्रतिसन्धाता प्रोक्तः पुरुषशब्दतः ।
... ...
प्रत्यक्षलक्षणाद्यं तु वक्तव्यं न्यायविस्तरे ।
इह तत् सूच्यतां मा वा पारम्पर्योपयोगतः ॥
—Seśvara-Mīmāṁsā.

disproving the identity of Ātman with the sense-organs and buddhi as well, and in the case, there will not be any necessity for depending on this sūtra.

Again, it is an accepted doctrine of the Seśvara-Mīmāṁsā that buddhi has no beginning: 'In the case of God as well as in the case of souls, cognition is eternal, arises of itself, extends over all things and is valid; but, its range is narrowed on account of various defect's.[1] How then can the Seśvara-Mīmāṁsā support the view that buddhi has a beginning? The author must either hold that the sūtra is erroneous or make some other interpretation. But, in any case, he cannot, with the help of this sūtra, establish the existence of an Ātman different from buddhi, etc.

The Mīmāṁsakas, on the other hand, hold this sūtra is intended to show that perception etc., cannot determine 'dharma'. According to them, this sūtra does not help us to establish the existence of a non-corporeal Ātman. Even the followers of Cārvāka who do not admit that there is a non-corporeal Ātman, do not find fault with this sūtra, for the word 'puruṣa' can very well mean a body endowed with intellect. There is nothing in the sūtra to contradict this meaning. Hence, it is not at all safe to conclude that Jaimini intends to establish the existence of a non-corporeal Ātman by means of this sūtra.

It is for this reason that Śabara Svāmin in his commentary on this sūtra, does not say anything about

---

1. ईश्वरस्येव जीवानामपि नित्यज्ञानं स्वतश्च सर्वविषयं प्रमात्मकञ्च, तत्तत्कर्मादिदोषवशात् सङ्कुचितविषयम्—Seśvara-Mīmāṁsā.

Ātman. He introduces the matter under the next sūtra : 'औत्पत्तिकस्तु' etc.,[1] in connection with the explanation of the portion 'अव्यतिरेकश्च'. This portion means that all statements of the Śruti are true. Śabara cites a text of the Śruti : 'the performer of a sacrifice goes to heaven'[1] and argues that as it is not possible for this body of flesh and blood to go to heaven, the existence of a non-corporeal Ātman is, therefore, implied. But, Śabara does not say that the idea follows directly from the letters of the sūtra; he gives a hint simply that it is borrowed by Jaimini from the Sūtras of Bādarāyaṇa because the name of Bādarayaṇa occurs in, the sūtra just after this portion. Śabara says that Jaimini mentions the name of Bādarāyṇa to pay respects to the latter; and, he implies thereby that this honour is shown by Jaimini with a view to acknowledging his debt to Bādarāyaṇa in this connection. We shall next proceed to show that all the famous expositors of the Sūtras and of the Bhāṣya are of opinion that the idea of the existence of a non-corporeal Ātman is borrowed from the Vedānta Sūtras.

Upavarṣa, the first Vṛttikāra of both the Pūrva and the Uttara Mīmāṁsā, states, when the question about the existence of Ātman arises in the Pūrva Mīmāṁsā, 'We shall speak about it in the Śārīraka'. Had he thought the matter to be contained in the Jaimini Sūtras, he would not have postponed the writing of his Vṛtti for the sake of another system.

1. Jaimini-Sūtra I. i. 5.

2. स एष यज्ञायुधी यजमानोऽञ्जसा स्वर्गं लोकं याति ।

We have seen already what the commentator Śabara has done. He does not, in fact, express any opinion regarding the derivation of the idea of a non-corporeal Ātman from the Sūtras of Bādarāyaṇa; but, it is only from the nature of his arguments that his position becomes clear and the interpretation of his expositor Kumārila will also testify to it. Thus states Kumārila in his Ślokavārttika :

'इत्याह नास्तिक्यनिराकरिष्णुरात्मास्तितां भाष्यकृदत्र युक्त्या ।
दृढत्वमेतद्विषयश्च बोधः प्रयाति वेदान्तनिषेवणेन ॥'[1]

'The commentator (Śabara), desirous of refuting atheism, says this about the existence of Ātman on the strength of arguments; and the knowledge of this matter will grow firm by studying the Vedānta'. So, according to Kumārila, Śabara bases his theory on arguments and not on the letters of the Sūtras of Jaimini. He also indicates that the Vedānta is the real source of this knowledge.

We next pass on to Śaṅkara. Let us quote here his words to understand his view with regard to this matter is :

'ननु शास्त्रप्रमुखे एव प्रथमे पादे शास्त्रफलोपभोगयोग्यस्य देहव्यतिरिक्तस्य आत्मनोऽस्तित्वमुक्तम् । सत्यमुक्तम् भाष्यकृता न तु तत्र आत्मास्तित्वे सूत्रमस्ति । इह तु स्वयमेव सूत्रकृता तदस्तित्वमाक्षेपपुरःसरं प्रतिष्ठापितम् । इत एवाकृष्याचार्येण शबरस्वामिना प्रमाणलक्षणे वर्णितम् । अतएव च भगवतीपवर्षेण प्रथमे तन्त्रे आत्मास्तित्वाभिधानप्रसक्तौ शारीरके वक्ष्याम इत्युद्धारः कृतः ।'

---

1. Ātmavāda, 148.

'One might say that iu the beginning of the Śāstra (Pūrva Mīmāṁsā) in the first pāda, the existence of an Ātman, which is different from the body and capable of enjoying the fruits mentioned in the Śruti, has been spoken of. It is true that the commentator (Śabara) has so held; but, there is no sūtra regarding the existence of Ātman. But, here (in the Vedānta) the author of the sūtras himself (Bādarāyaṇa) establishes that systematically. It is from this sūtra[1] that Śabara Svāmin has borrowed what he has stated in connection with his definition of valid cognition. It is for this reason that when the question about the existence of an Ātman arises, the revered Upavarṣa says : 'We shall speak about it in the Śārīraka.'

According to Śaṅkarācārya, the Pūrva Mīmāṁsā and Uttara Mīmāṁsā are different systems; so he might say without any hesitation that the conception of a non-corporeal Ātman follows from the Sūtras of Jaimini; for, if the same thing be treated in two different systems there will be no repetition. But, the Seśvara-Mīmāṁsakas regard the two systems as one concrete whole. If they say that the existence of a non-corporeal Ātman has been established twice in the same system (once by Jaimini and again by Bādarāyaṇa) they will accuse Bādarāyaṇa of having made a useless repetition. Such a charge against a Sūtrakāra is anything but fair. To safeguard the importance of the sūtra 'एक आत्मनः शरीरे भावात्' of Bādarāyaṇa they ought to consider that the conception does not follow from the

1. एक आत्मनः शरीरे भावात् . Vedanta-Sūtra III. iii. 53.

Sūtras of Jaimini. But, instead of doing that, the Seśvara-Mīmāṁsakas have tried to adopt a middle course. They say that from the Sūtras of Jaimini we learn that there is an Ātman capable of going to heaven, and that from the Sūtras of Bādarāyaṇa we learn that Ātman is eternal :

'पारलौकिकतामात्रमिह तावदपेक्षितम् ।
शारीरके तु नित्यत्वं वाच्यं नित्यफलार्थिना ॥'[1]

This does not at all seem to be a reasonable solution. Such a distinction between नित्य and पारलौकिक as drawn here is futile; for, it is absurd to imagine that Ātman is capable of transmigration without first admitting that it is eternal. It is for this reason that Kumārila, while enumerating the attributes of Ātman, asserts at the outset that it is eternal, and then goes on to say that it is capable of assuming other bodies i.e., fit for other worlds :

'नित्यः सर्वगतः पुमान् । देहान्तरक्षमः कल्प्यः ॥'[2]

It becomes clear, therefore, that all these great exponents, Upavarṣa, Śabara, Kumārila and Śaṅkarācārya are at one in holding that the existence of a non-corporeal Ātman is not established by the Sūtras of Jaimini. The arguments put forward by the Seśvara-

1. Seśvara-Mīmāṁsā.

2. ज्ञानशक्तिस्वभावोऽतो नित्यः सर्वगतः पुमान् ।
देहान्तरक्षमः कल्प्यः सोऽगच्छन्नेव योक्ष्यते ॥ --Ātmavāda 73.
... ...
सत्ताज्ञानादिरूपाणां कर्ता तावत् स्वयं पुमान् । Loc. cit 76.

Mīmāṁsā are not strong enough to justify any departure on our part from these great authorities.

We shall now pass on to note the attributes of Ātman as enumerated by Kumārila.

Ātman, according to Kumārila, is : (1) self-illumined; (2) the permanent and persistent notion of 'I' (consciousness); (3) the object of the cognition of 'I' (अहंवित्तिः); (4) the basis of cognition, emotion etc., which are nothing but particular conditions of its own; (5) eternal; (6) omnipresent; and (7) capable of doing and enjoying things.

IS ĀTMAN SELF-ILLUMINED ?

As regards the self-luminosity of Ātman, Kumārila says :

'आत्मनैव प्रकाश्योऽयमात्मा ज्योतिरितीरितम् ।
अग्राह्य इति सामान्यात् सर्वेणेति प्रतीयते ॥
आत्मज्योतिष्ट्ववचनात् परैरित्यवतिष्ठते ।
... ...
आत्मज्ञानाविनाभूतदृष्टचेष्टानिरूपणात् ।
परेषामात्मविज्ञानमनुमानादुदाहृतम् ॥'[1]

'It is stated that Ātman is a light which illumines itself. The epithet अग्राह्य apparently means that it is imperceptible to all; but, as the Śruti says that it is आत्मज्योति (self-illumined), we conclude that it is imperceptible only to others (and not to itself). Seeing the efforts (of a person) which cannot take place without the existence of an Ātman, others infer that he possesses an Ātman'.

1. Ātmavāda 142-45.

If we take the expression अग्राह्य in the sense stated above, we shall have no difficulty in understanding the text of the Śruti, 'अगृह्यो न हि गृह्यते'.

This clearly shows that Dr. Jha does not correctly represent Kumārila when he states, : 'Kumārila holds that the soul is not self-luminous but known by mental perception (Śāstradīpikā p. 101)".[1] Dr. Jha cites Śāstradīpikā as his authority. There is, indeed, a passage in the Śāstradīpikā where it is stated thus : 'If Ātman were self-luminous, it would shine in deep sleep also; but, it does not shine at that time, etc.'; but, the author of the Śāstradīpikā is there trying to refute the arguments of the Advaitins who hold that the object of the cognition of 'I' is not Ātman. Had it really been his intention to deny the self-luminosity of Ātman as understood by the Bhāṭṭas, then he would certainly have criticised the passage of the Śloka-vārttika, 'आत्मनैव प्रकाश्योऽयं'. Nowhere does Kumārila say that Ātman is not luminous during deep sleep.

In the course of criticising the view that the cause of pleasure is thought of at the time of enjoying the pleasure, Kumārila says, 'अपरामृश्यमाने तु स्वापकाले सुखाश्रये'[2] where the expression सुखाश्रये might lead to some confusion with regard to its actual meaning; for, it seems apparently to mean the substratum of pleasure, etc., i.e., Ātman; and, so the whole passage seems to mean : 'during deep sleep Ātman is not thought of, i.e., it does not shine'. But, here, the question of Ātman cannot arise at all. Ātman may, indeed, be the substratum of

1. Indian Thought, Vol. II. p. 254.
2. Ātmavāda, 18.

pleasure; but, it is by no means the cause of pleasure. We learn from the context that the discussion is about the enjoyment of pleasure and not about the cause of it; and, Ātman, therefore, has nothing to do with it. Let us now see in what sense the Nyāyaratnākara takes the expression सुखाश्रय. This expression implies, according to this commentary, that which gives comfort, i.e., bedding etc. The whole passage means, therefore, that in deep sleep, bedding and such other implements of pleasure are not thought of; in deep sleep, pleasure itself is enjoyed, though the instruments of pleasure are not thought of. So, it is clear, that in deep sleep pleasure itself is enjoyed, though the instruments of pleasure are not thought of. But, unless Ātman is shining at that time, how can the enjoyment be possible? So, according to Kumārila, Ātman is shining at that time.

Now, Pārthasārathi Miśra, the author of the Nyāyaratnākara, also, happens to be the writer of the Śāstradīpikā. If he does not find any passage in the Vārttika indicating that Ātman is not self-illumined, how can he state in his Śāstradīpikā that Atman is not so? It only proves that he does not correctly represent the view of Kumārila in his Śāstradīpikā although he says in his introduction to the work 'कुमारिलमतेनाहं करिष्ये शास्त्रदीपिकाम्' 'I shall write this Śāstradīpikā in accordance with the views of Kumārila'.

Let us now ascertain the Prābhākara view on this point. In the Nyāyavivaraṇa there is a pūrva-pakṣa which proceeds on the assumption that Ātman is self-illumined. The author of the Nyāyasuddhā has taken this view for the view of Prabhākara. But, the author of the Mādhva-tātparya-candrikā[1] notices that this pūrva-pakṣa in the Nyāyavivaraṇa is not in accordance with the view of Prabhākara, as the self-luminosity of Ātman is never admitted by Prabhākara. The Gururājīya[2] which is a commentary on the Candrikā says on the same point : 'according to Prabhākara, cognition is self-luminous and Ātman is only the basis of cognition. Had the pūrva-pakṣa meant to follow Prabhākara, it would have taken its stand on that ground and not on the self-luminosity of Ātman which is never admitted by Prabhākara'. Thus, we see that according to these eminent writers the Ātman of Prabhākara is not self-illumined, and that, when one of them—the author of the Nyāyasudhā—makes a contrary statement, the others are pointing it out. Dr. Jha accepts this view as that propounded in the Prakaraṇa-pañcikā. We quote here his very words : 'Thus, then, according to Prabhākara the soul is not self-illumined.........it is cognition alone that is so.[3] Dr. Keith also restates the very same view : 'In the view of Prabhākara cognition is self-illumined, but this doctrine is not applicable to the soul".[4]

ĀTMAN AS CONSCIOUSNESS AND AN OBJECT OF COGNITION

Ātman, again, is described in the Ślokavārttika as ज्ञानशक्तिस्वभावः i e., of the nature of consciousness. In the

1. A work of the Mādhva school.
2. A work by Vyāsarāja.
3. Indian Thought, Vol. II. p. 252.
4. Karma-Mīmāṁsā, p. 79.

Siddhāntabindu of Madhusūdana Sarasvatī, we find the passage : 'जडो बोधात्मकश्च इति भाट्टाः'.[1] 'the Bhāṭṭas hold that Ātman is जड (object of cognition) and of the nature of consciousness'. This passage has been thus explained in the Nyāyaratnāvalī—आत्मनोऽस्ति अंशत्रयं चिदंशोऽचिदंशश्च चिदंशेन द्रष्टृत्वम्......अचिदंशेन ज्ञानसुखादिपरिणामित्वं मामहं जानामि इति ज्ञेयत्वञ्च.

'Ātman has two parts, one of which is चित् (conscious) and the other अचित् . By its conscious part, it is the cogniser and by the other part, it tranforms itself into cognition, emotion, etc. and becomes the object of the experience 'I know myself'. From this it clearly appears that the Bhāṭṭas have been represented as holding that Ātman is consciousness. From the Nyāyaratnāvalī we also learn that the attributes, जडत्व (object of cognition) and consciousness, are not contradictory because Ātman is conscious by virtue of its चित् part and is जड (object of cognition) by virtue of its अचित् part. In the Siddhāntabindu, the Prābhākara view is thus stated : कर्ता भोक्ता जडो विभुरिति प्राभाकराः; the Prābhākaras hold that Ātman is the agent, the enjoyer, जड and omnipresent. The word जड is explained in the Nyāyaratnāvalī as follows : स च ज्ञानस्वरूपभिन्नत्वाज् जडः, जानामीति ज्ञानाश्रयत्वेन स भाति, न ज्ञानरूपत्वेन'—'and he is said to be jaḍa, because he is different from consciousness; he appears as the substratum of the cognition, 'I know' but not as consciousness'.

In the Bhāṣya, Śabara Svāmīn has propounded : 'ज्ञानातिरिक्तः स्थायी ज्ञाता वर्तते'—'there is a permanent cogniser apart from ज्ञान'. This raises a doubt as to

1. Kumbhakoṇa ed. p. 59.

whether Śabara, by thus distinguishing the cogniser from ज्ञान, denies the identity of Ātman with consciousness. But, Śabara refutes here the theory of Transient Cognitions (क्षणिकविज्ञानवाद) and does not assail the theory of Permanent Consciousness (स्थिरविज्ञानवाद) at all. In the atheistic Darśanas there is a theory that an Ātman is nothing but a single cognition; and as the acts of cognition are numerous, these Darśanas hold that there are numerous Ātmans. Thus ,an Ātman, according to them, is merely a technical name for an act of cognition, and does not mean anything which is permanent or eternal. Śabara contends that if each Ātman be a separate cognition, there will be no connection or association between one Ātman and another (i.e., between the cogniser and the rememberer), because it will disappear as soon as it takes place. And, hence, the recollection of things will be impossible and so forth. By the word ज्ञान Śabara means this sort of Ātman or cognition. He holds that behind these short cognitions, there is a permanent cogniser, i.e. consciousness. We, thus, see that the Bhāṣyakāra does not refute स्थिरविज्ञानवाद; and, consequently, he is not against the view that Ātman is consciousness.

The Bhāṣya says again : 'स्वसंवेद्यः स भवति, नासावन्येन शक्यते द्रष्टुं दर्शयितुं वा ।' 'It (Ātman) is known by itself, it is incapable of being seen or shown by others'. This statement can be cogent only if we take Ātman to be of the nature of consciousness.

Again, in the following passage of the Śāstradīpikā, we find that three distinct attributes of Ātman are recognised :

'इति सिद्धः शरीरादिव्यतिरिक्तो मानसप्रत्यक्षरूपोऽहंप्रत्यय-गम्यो ज्ञाता। कथं पुनर्ज्ञातुर्ज्ञेयत्वम्?'

'The cogniser is something different from the body, etc.; it is consciousness (the notion of 'I') and the object of the cognition of 'I'. But, how is it that the cogniser itself becomes the object of cognition ?' This view is undisputedly quite in agreement with that of the Bhāṭṭas. The author of the Śāstradīpikā does not only say that Ātman is the basis of cognition and the object of the cognition of 'I', but that it is consciousness (the notion of 'I') also. Dr. Jha, while stating the attributes of Ātman, has omitted to mention that Ātman is consciousness, : 'He (Kumārila) holds the soul to be either the substratum, or the object of the notion of 'I'.[1] Probably, Dr. Jha has accepted the reading that is found in the Benaras edition of the books : 'मानसप्रत्यक्षरूपाहंप्रत्ययगम्यो ज्ञाता'[2]. In this reading the expression मानसप्रत्यक्षरूप is a part of the compound and qualifies अहंप्रत्यय; so, it is not a separate adjective and does not qualify ज्ञाता. From this reading we do not get that Ātman is consciousness (the notion of 'I') . Now, let us see how the Yukti-sneha-prapūraṇī,[3] a commentary on the Śāstradīpikā, interprets it.

It proceeds to explain the text 'कथं पुनर्ज्ञातुर्ज्ञेयत्वम् ?' with the following words, 'गूढाभिसन्धिः पृच्छति' 'in asking the question the author has something in his mind.' The text is plain enough; why then should the author have something in his mind ? The commentatoı gives a full

1. Indian Thought, Volume II, page 254.
2. Śāstradīpikā pp. 347.
3. p. 122.

explanation of it in his सिद्धान्तचन्द्रिकागूढार्थविवरण, a commentary which he himself has written on his Yukti-sneha-prapūraṇī. There he says,—आत्मनि ज्ञेयत्वे विषयतया ज्ञानत्वानुपपत्तिरित्यभिसन्धिः : 'If Ātman is a thing that is known, it will be the object of cognition, and then its attribute of consciousness will be untenable;—this is what the author (of the Śāstradīpikā) has in his mind'. Now, the question about the untenability of Ātman's attribute as consciousness would never arise in the author's mind, unless he admitted it before. But, according to the reading of the Benares edition, this becomes impossible. The Bombay edition, on the other hand, reads 'मानसप्रत्यक्षरूपः।' This is a separate adjective and qualifies ज्ञाता; and, so, it supplies the other attribute of Ātman, namely, consciousness. This reading, therefore, is consistent with the remarks of the author of the Yukti-sneha-prapūraṇī, and should be regarded as the correct reading. Thus, we see that, according to the Śāstradīpikā, Ātman is the notion of 'I', the object of the cognition of 'I' and the basis of eognition.

It is true that the Śāstradīpikā has, after an elaborate discussion, come to the conclusion that Ātman is not consciousness[1]; but it has done so only to refute the view of the Advaitins that Ātman is consciousness, pure and simple; and, in fact, it can never be the intention of the Śāstradīpikā to refute the view of the Bhāṭṭas who hold that Ātman is both जड as well as of the nature of consciousness. It might, however, be still contended that there is practically no difference

1. Bombay Edition, p. 129.

between the Bhāṭṭas and the Advaitins in this respect, because, according to the Advaitins also, there is some sort of darkness (जडत्व) covering Ātman. But, in reply to this, it may be urged that the जडत्व of the Advaitins is an imposed one, and not real; and surely, the author of the Śāstradīpikā does not deem it necessary to enter into a discussion about the reality or unreality of that जडत्व in a work of Mīmāṁsā. As a Mīmāṁsaka he cannot but admit that there is जडत्व in Ātman; but, he cannot declare—be he ever so inclined to do so—that Ātman is nothing but consciousness; for, such a conclusion would give rise to a confusion in the minds of the ordinary people who are fond of karman. As a Mīmāṁsaka, therefore, he has refuted the view of the Advaitins only; and, that he has refuted no other view is clear from the very context of his discussion.

As regards the Prābhākara view of Ātman as an object of cognition, Dr. Jha says : 'Kumārila holds that the soul is not self-luminous, but is known by mental perception which latter fact Prabhākara denies'. This 'latter fact' undoubtedly means the cognition of Ātman by mental perception. But, we should point out here that the statement of Dr. Jha goes against the Prakaraṇa-pañcikā. True it is, that according to the Prābhākaras Ātman enters into all cognitions of external things; but, they do not mean that Ātman is never cognised independently of the cognition of external things. This sort of cognition of Ātman which concerns Ātman alone (निर्विकल्पक), is acknowledged by them. The Prakaraṇa-pañcikā states that all cognitions of external things (सविकल्पक) are preceded by a cognition of Ātman (निर्विकल्पक); that, although the cognition of Ātman has always been existing, still it has not been existing in connection with the external thing perceived; and that, therefore, the cognition of an external thing takes place according to the principle of continuous cognitions (धारावाहिक न्याय).[1] The cognition of Ātman in the shape, 'I know myself' exists permanently within a man. When he sees an external thing, such as a book, his cognition is of the shape, 'I know this book', i.e., he knows that there is his self and that there is the book as well. It may now be asked : if the cognition of the self be permanently present in us, the self is a thing already known; why then, should one know it afresh, i.e., have a fresh cognition of the self when one perceives an external thing ? To this it may be answered that though undoubtedly the self is a thing already known, still it is not known in connection with the particular thing perceived. For the sake of this connection, therefore, a particular cognition of the self is necessary. The principle of continuous cognitions may be cited here to explain this. I see a stick once, twice, thrice, and so on; one might contend that there should be no cognition of the stick when I see it for the second time, etc., because it is a thing already known to me by virtue of its having been seen before. But, there is actually a cognition each time the stick is presented to my eyes. When I see it for the second time, I do know that I see it a second time; when I see

1. आत्मनः प्रमातृत्वान् निर्विकल्पकपृष्ठभाविनश्च सविकल्पकस्य गृहीत-ग्राहित्वेऽपि धारावाहिकन्यायेन प्रामाण्यं वेदितव्यम् ॥

Prakaraṇa-pañcikā, p. 56.

it for the third time, I do know that I see it for the third time; and so on. Each succeeding occasion is a new occasion; and, in connection with each new occasion, we have really a fresh cognition of the thing presented. This is known as the principle of continuous cognitions.

Thus, we see that according to the Prābhākaras Ātman is known by mental perception. The Prakaraṇa-pañcikā does not only assert this; but, it also gives a sufficient description of the relation that subsists between सविकल्पक and निर्विकल्पक cognitions.[1]

ĀTMAN AS THE BASIS OF COGNITION

According to the Bhāṭṭas, Ātman is the substratum of cognition which is nothing but a product of Ātman. Rāmānuja also accepts this view of the Bhāṭṭas. But, according to Rāmānuja, cognition which is an attribute of Ātman is eternal and is capable of expansion and contraction;[2] while, the Bhāṭṭas hold that cognition is a product (परिणाम) of Ātman, which arises through pramāṇas (the means of knowledge). As regards the view that cognition is caused by pramāṇas, there is no difference between the Bhāṭṭas, the Naiyāyikas and the Vaiśeṣikas. According to the Prābhākaras, also, cognition is a product of Ātman. So, the Prakaraṇa-pañcikā states: 'Cognition of objects is temporary. Here Ātman is the constituent cause and the contact of Ātman with manas is an auxiliary

---

1. Benares ed. page 56.
2. Seśvara Mīmāṁsā Darśana.

cause.'[1] Ātman is said to be a constituent cause because it converts itself into a particular state called cognition. The Naiyāyikas and the Vaiśeṣikas have accepted 'ārambhavāda'[2]; and, hence, it is not necessary for them to hold that cognition is a product of Ātman. There is another point of difference also. According to the Naiyāyikas and the Vaiśeṣikas, Ātman is illumined by cognition and one cognition is illumined by another cognition. Thus, they do not recognise that cognition is self-illumined. The Prābhākaras do not believe in the self-luminosity of Ātman but believe in that of cognition. We shall see, later on, that Prābhākaras are not all unanimous on this point. According to some of them, three things appear in a cognition, cognition itself, Ātman and the object (त्रिपुटीभानम् .)[3] Kumārila, however, differs from this view. According to him, Ātman is self-illumined; and, so, it is not to be cognised in the cognition of objects, and cognition itself is inferred. It is only the objects, therefore, that appear in a cognition. Kumārila does not recognise the self-luminosity of cognition, because he contends that if cognition itself be self-luminous, the objects will appear as pure manifestations of the cognition and will not exist as real objects and conse-

---

1. 'विषयावबोधस्तावत् कादाचित्को दृश्यते तस्य चात्मा समवायिकारणम्......................बाह्यरूपादिग्रहे च सन्निकर्षचतुष्टयं कारणम्, आत्मनः सन्निकर्षः...................' Prakaraṇa Pañcikā, pp. 52-3.

2. An effect not already in existence is produced through the activity of causes which are existing.

3. Prakaraṇa-pañcikā, pp. 152-3.

quently, there will remain no difference between this view and Vijñāna-vāda.[1] It is really very difficult to see how the Prābhākaras will justify the independent existence of objects if they maintain the self-luminosity of cognition.

Though the Bhāṭṭas hold that Ātman is the substratum of cognition, they never admit that it is the substratum of the 'I' element in cognition. But, Prof. Keith in his 'Karma-Mīmāṁsā' says: 'The soul he (Kumārila) holds to be the substratum of the 'I' element in cognition; and, this appears to be practically identical with Prabhākara's view that the soul is the substratum of the self-illumined cognition and the 'I' element in it'[2] Now, we must examine whether the Bhāṭṭa view is practically identical with that of the Prābhākaras in this respect, as Prof. Keith holds it to be. If, indeed, the Bhāṭṭas held that Ātman is cognised in the cognition of external objects, the above statement, 'this appears to be practically identical with Prabhākara's view,' would have been correct. But, the Bhāṭṭa view is directly antagonistic to it. Kumārila has contended, as we have seen above, that in case of cognition being regarded as self-illumined the reality of external objects becomes untenable. In the face of this contention, we cannot be justified in holding that the two views are practically identical.

---

1. Śūnya-vāda, 233.

2. Karma-Mīmāṁsā, p. 71.

We may discuss the matter a little more fully. Why do the Prābhākaras hold that three things, cognition, Ātman and the object, appear in the cognition of an external object ? Cognition, in general, does not always involve these three elements. We have already seen that even the Prābhākaras admit that there is an independent cognition of Ātman. But, in that cognition, no external object is present. So, the third element is wanting there. If they have propounded this view to justify such uses, as, 'I know this book', etc., made by a man while perceiving a book, it must be said that they have failed; for, cognition which is self-illumined, does not want itself to be its own object for its own use. The cogniser, too, which is a constituent cause of cognition, does not appear directly; but, such uses as are mentioned above are possible, because the presence of Ātman is implicitly understood there just in the same way as the existence of earth which is its constituent cause is understood in the perception of an earthen jar. So, it is useless to hold that these two elements appear as distinct objects of cognition.

Hence, we see that the doctrine of the Appearance of Three Elements, Tripuṭībhānam, of the new school of Prābhākaras does not rest on a firm ground. It is for this reason that the author of the Nyāyaratnāvalī says that the old school of the Prābhākaras does not propound such a doctrine. In tbe Nyāyaratnāvalī, it is plainly stated that the old school of the Prābhākaras does not admit that cognition and the cogniser are the objects of cognition, as our uses are possible by virtue of identity (तादात्म्य) and inherence (समवाय) respectively.[1]

The renowned Mīmāṁsaka, Murāri Miśra, has, however, taken a different view on this point. He, too, does not accept the doctrine of त्रिपुटीभान. According to him, there arises, at first, a cognition of the 'jar', the knowledge in the shape 'I know the jar', which is followed by अनुव्यवसाय. So, Murāri Miśra holds that the knowledge of cognition is an after-effect of cognition itself. This view is to be gathered from Mathurānātha's famous commentary on the Tattva-cintāmaṇi[2] as no work of the author is available now-a-days. It is clear, then, that he is neither a follower of the new school of the Prābhākaras as he does not accept त्रिपुटीभान; nor, can he be said to be a follower of the Bhāṭṭa school simply because he does not hold that cognition is known by inference. His adumbration of अनुव्यवसाय is strikingly original. We have just now stated on the authority of the Nyāyaratnāvali that त्रिपुटीभान was not accepted by the old school of the Prābhākaras; but, no indication of the existence of any such doctrine as अनुव्यवसाय in that school can be obtained. Mathurānātha states the view of the Prābhākaras as follows: 'गुरुमते अयं घट इति व्यवसाय एव' : in the view of Guru there is cognition in the shape : 'this is a jar'. It is evident that he refers to the view of the old school of the Prābhākaras. So, practically, there are three different views on this point : the first is the doctrine of त्रिपुटीभान of the new school of the Prābhākaras ; the second

1. Kumbhakona ed. p. 18.

2. Bib. Ind. Pratyakṣa-khaṇḍa p. 151.

view (of the Bhāṭṭas and the old school of the Prābhākaras) accepts neither त्रिपुटीभान nor अनुव्यवसाय, while the third accepts अनुव्यवसाय. This new course adopted dy Murāri is probably responsible for the proverb, 'मुरारेस्तृतीयः पन्थाः'.

Thus, at length, we see that the conclusion of Kumārila is that the cognition of Ātman takes place only in the inner perception of Ātman and not in the cognition of external things. So, he says in the Śloka-vārttika :

'अहं वेद्मीत्यहंबुद्धिर्ज्ञातारमधिगच्छति ।'

'The consciousness, 'I know', refers to the cogniser'. It becomes clear, therefore, that Ātman, according to Kumārila, is cognised without the cognition of external things, or, in other words, Ātman is not to be described as 'the substratum of the 'I' element in cognition', as Prof. Keith puts it.

THE PRĀBHĀKARA VIEW FURTHER INVESTIGATED

Both the Bhāṭṭas and the Prābhākaras admit that cognition is a product (परिणाम) of Ātman; but, while the former hold that cognition is an object of inference, the latter are of opinion, as has been stated by various writers, that it is self-illumined. Now, the question arises as to whether the self-luminosity of cognition is actually admitted by the Prābhākaras. Prabhākara, while explaining the passage—अर्थविषया हि प्रत्यक्षबुद्धिर्न बुद्धिविषया[1] (it is the object that is perceived and not the cognition), says in the Bṛhatī : अतः सिद्धमानुमानिकत्वं बुद्धेः फलतः; thus, it is established that cognition is a matter of

1. Śabara-Bhāṣya, Ben. ed. p. 9.

inference[1]. Śālikanātha, too, suggests in the Prakaraṇa-pañcikā that there are two kinds of cognition, one of which is an object of inference and the other self-illumined : किं तर्ह्यनुमीयते ज्ञानम् ? ननु न तत् संवित् स्वयम्प्रकाशाया भिन्नमुपलभ्यते ? सत्यम्, अतएवानुमीयते । ननु किं तदिति ? न तद् विद्मः । संविदुत्पत्तिकारणमन्तःकरणसन्निकर्षस्य तदित्यवगम्य परितुष्यतामायुष्मता ।[2] What, then, is that cognition which is inferred ? No such thing as is different from the self-illumined saṁvit is perceived ? True; and, therefore, it is inferred. Now, what is it ? We do not know; you may be satisfied to learn that it is the same thing as the contact of the अन्तःकरण (inner organ of sense) which gives rise to the saṁvit'. It seems that this self-illumined saṁvit of Śālikanātha is consciousness and that the contact of the अन्तःकरण (inner organ of sense), which is an object of inference, is cognition.

The Vedāntins use the word vṛtti to denote that side of the antaḥkaraṇa which is connected with an external object and which causes reflections of the hidden consciousness. Most probably, it is this contact of the antaḥkaraṇa which is meant in the passage of the Prakaraṇa-pañcikā cited above. Taken in this light, the only difference between the Vedānta view and the Mīmāṁsā view would be that the Vedāntins would regard vṛtti as a product (pariṇāma) of the antaḥkaraṇa whereas the Mīmāṁsakas would regard it as a product of Ātman. With the Vedāntins it is important to see that Ātman is unaffected; and, so, they cannot

---

1. Bṛhatī p. 87.
2. Prakaraṇa-pañcikā p. 63.

admit that Ātman has any pariṇāma; the Mīmāṁsakas, on the other hand, are devoted to karman; and, so they cannot introduce into the Mīmāṁsā, the view of the Vedānta that the expressions, 'I', 'mine', etc, indicate misconceptions of Ātman. This is clearly borne out by the following passage of the Bṛhatī :

'यदुक्तमहङ्कारममकारावनात्मन्यात्माभिमानाविति, मृदितकषायाणामेवैतत् कथनीयं न कर्मसङ्गिनाम्। आह च भगवान् द्वैपायनो न बुद्धिभेदं जनयेदज्ञानां कर्मसङ्गिनामिति रहस्याधिकारे।'[1]

'The statement that the expressions 'I', 'mine', etc., indicate a misconception of Ātman should be made to those who have subdued that attachment to worldly objects and not before those who like to stick to karman; and, the great Dvaipāyana has said 'You must not create a confusion in the minds of ignorant people who are attached to karman'.

The knowledge of the true nature of Ātman as free from अहङ्कार and ममकार is prejudicial to the cause of sacrificial performances; and, hence, the Mīmāṁsakas do not prefer it. We find here exactly the same thing stated briefly by Prabhākara as is stated at great length by Śaṅkarācārya in his adhyāsa-bhāṣya.

Now, we should ascertain here the meaning of the word, saṁvit, which is nowhere clearly defined in the Mīmāṁsā text-books. The extract from the Bṛhatī just quoted seems to imply that saṁvit is really to be regarded as a form of Ātman. In the Prakaraṇa-pañcikā, we find that both saṁvit and Ātman have been characterised as self-illumined'. We have already

1. Bṛhatī, p. 256.

cited the passage in which saṁvit is so described and here we quote the other passage which describes Ātman in a similar way : 'मानसं प्रत्यक्षं सुखादिष्विवात्मन्यपि प्रमाणमिति केचिदाहुः । तदयुक्तमिति प्राभाकरवराः, स्वयम्प्रकाशत्वेन विषयप्रतीतिगोचरत्वेन तदुपपत्तेः'[1] 'there are some who preach that Ātman, like pleasure, etc., is known by mental perception; but, the revered Prābhākaras think that this view is not reasonable. Ātman is known because it is self-illumined and because it is involved in the cognition of external things'. This goes to establish that saṁvit is identical with Ātman.

But, Prabhākara is unwilling to introduce this idea into the Mīmāṁsā. His attitude is clearly understood from the following passage of the Bṛhatī :

'प्रमातृरूपता च ज्ञानस्यानाशङ्कनीयैव, अनाशङ्कितत्वात्; युक्तञ्चेदं नाशङ्कितं कर्मप्रवणत्वात् ।[2]

'It should not be supposed that jñāna is pramātṛ (cogniser); for, such a supposition has never been made; and, it is quite in the fitness of things that it has not been made for they are fond of karman'. Thus, we see that though Prabhākara has every respect for the Vedānta doctrine, he is still uuwilling to promulgate it in the Mīmāṁsā. He, however, thinks it proper to characterise Ātman as the substratum of jñāna which is a prodnct of itself; and, so, he says in the Bṛhatī :

इह तु सर्वज्ञेयप्रमातृतयैव संविदुपन्यस्ता ।[3]

'In the Mīmāṁsā, saṁvit is to be regarded as the cogniser of all objects of cognition'.

---

1. Prakaraṇa-pañcikā, p. 151.
2. Bṛhatī p. 254.
3. Op. cit. p. 243.

In this passage saṁvit, being characterised as प्रमातृ, is distinguished from cognition; and, so the whole passage is to be taken as implying that Ātman, which is the substratum of cognition (an object of inference) is saṁvit (consciousness). Ātman is the substratum of cognition which is an object of inference but not the substratum of any self-illumined cognition. That this is the conclusion of Prabhākara appears from the following passage of the Bṛhatī :

यदपि ज्ञातृतैव ज्ञानादृते न शक्यते वक्तुमिति.................
तदपि प्रत्युक्तं कामं विज्ञानमपह्नूयते नार्थं इति ।[1]

'If it be said that ज्ञातृत्व is not possible without ज्ञान the answer would be that we may rather suppress ज्ञान than objects'.

Here, we see that the suppression of cognition is regarded as preferable to the suppression of objects. This sort of preference could never have been given to objects if cognition had been regarded as self-illumined. So, we think that cognition is regarded here as an object of inference, as is evident from the following passage of the Bhāṣya : 'अर्थविषया हि प्रत्यक्षबुद्धिर्न बुद्धिविषया'; otherwise, the above statement of the Bṛhatī would be meaningless. We see, therefore, that the conclusion, that according to Prabhākara, Ātman is the substratum of self-illumined cognition, is untenable even though it finds favour with many authors.

Thus, we see that saṁvit (consciousness) is self-illumined and is the same thing as the cogniser, i.e. Ātman. We also know that cognition is a product of

1. Bṛhatī p. 254.

Ātman (pariṇāma) and is not Ātman itself. Cognition is not, therefore, the same thing as saṁvit (consciousness).

The passage of the Bṛhatī 'संवित्तयैव हि संवित् संवेद्या भवति न संवेद्यतया' is, thus, translated by Prof. Keith : 'As expounded by Prabhākara, consciousness (saṁvit) which is self-illumined is cognised, but not as an object of cognition; but, as cognition'.[1] He has translated the word 'saṁvit' as consciousness; but, he has taken the word 'saṁvedya' as meaning 'an object of cognition'. But, it seems better to render the passage thus : Consciousness is cognised but not as an object of consciousness. By saying that consciousness is not an object of consciousness, it is meant that it is an object of cognition. There is another passage in the Bṛhatī which states this clearly : 'संवित् न संवेद्या किन्तु प्रमेया'. A distinction between the cognition of an external object and that of consciousness is expressed here. An object is both prameya and saṁvedya whereas consciousness is only prameya. That which is an object of vṛtti or cognition is prameya; and, that which is connected with consciousness of saṁvedya. To safeguard an independent existence of external objects, the Bhāṭṭas deny the self-luminosity of cognition; and so the passage : 'एकसंवेद्यविषयैव ह्येका संविदन्न संवेद्यद्वयविषया' of the Bṛhatī means, 'at one time, saṁvit connects itself with one object and not two'. Now, as consciousness or saṁvit is self-illumined, so pramāṇas cannot give rise to it; but, pramāṇas give rise to vṛtti or cognition; and, when vṛtti arises, consciousness shines or becomes reflected.

1. Karma-Mīmāṁsā, p. 20.

This view is the same as that of the Advaitins. It also indicates that no appearance of external objects is possible without a connection with consciousness. We should notice that here the Mīmāṁsaka touches on the Vedānta doctrine that there is no separate existence of the phenomenal world as apart from the existence of Ātman. Prabhākara, however, who is a supporter of sacrifices, cannot go so far as to substantiate it plainly; but, still he says in the Bṛhatī :

'यदि परं ब्रह्मविदामेष निश्चयो यदुपलभ्यते तदसत्यम्, यच्चोपलभ्यते तत् तत्त्वमिति, नमस्तेभ्यः। विदुषि नोत्तरं वाच्यम्।'[1] 'But, if this be the conclusion of those who know Brahman that all that is known is false and that which is not known is true, I bow to them (i.e., I do not challenge their conclusion); no opposition should be made against wise men'. From this, it clearly appears that at heart, Prabhākara was not opposed to the Vedāntins; but, he could not openly accept their doctrines. We have said before that, if the Prābhākaras regard cognition as self-illumined, it would be difficult for them to avert Vijñāna-vāda. But, if the conclusion which we now arrive at be accepted, Vijñāna-vāda will be easily averted. The difference between Vijñāna-vāda and this view of the Prābhākaras is that, according to the Vijñānavāda, all external objects are forms of vṛtti which is momentary, whereas, according to this view, the objects are connected with consciousness through the medium of vṛtti. So, the Vijñāna-vada does not stand in the way.

1. Bṛhatī, p. 239.

Here, we should also notice the difference that exists between the Bhāṭṭa view and the Vijñāna-vāda. Saṁvit is known by the Vaijñānikas as ālaya-vijñāna and vṛtti as pravṛtti-vijñāna. Now, if the Vaijñānikas admit that ālaya-vijñāna is a permanent thing, that external objects are objects of the vijñānas and that pravṛtti-vijñāna is the product of ālaya-vijñāna, there would be no difference between the Bhāṭṭa theory and the Vijñānavāda. In the view of the Bhāṭṭas, there is an unconscious counterpart (अचिदंश) of consciousness (Ātman) which may be regarded as the same thing as the antaḥkaraṇa and by means of which Ātman is transformed into the shape of vṛtti. But, the Vaijñānikas do not admit the existence of such a counterpart, Hence, it is not possible for them to hold that pravṛtti-vijñāna is a product ālaya-vijñāna. Thus, in the Bhāṭṭa view, Ātman is treated as jaḍa or prameya. What will, then, be the distinction between Ātman and an ordinary thing ? The answer is that unlike other things Ātman is not saṁvedya (object of consciousness). It is, therefore, regarded as consciousness. So, they say that in the Bhāṭṭa view Ātman is both jaḍa and consciousness. This is, also, the purport of the passage : 'संवित्तयैव हि संवित् संवेद्या............'

So, we see that in the Prābhākara view, too, cognition is an object of inference and consciousness (Ātman) is self-illumined. There is, then, no difference between the Prābhākara view and the Bhāṭṭa view in this respect. But, the Prābhākara view is not so represented by the author of the Mādhava-tātparya-candrikā and other writers. We do not understand why it is so. The author of the Nyāyaratnāvalī asserts on the authority of the Tattva-cintāmaṇi that there were two schools of the Prābhākaras, one old and the other new; and, that the older school did not accept the doctrine of tripuṭībhāna.[1] It is probable that the view which we have set forth above was the view of the old school of the Prābhākaras.

ĀTMAN IS ETERNAL

According to Rāmānuja, cognition is an attribute of Ātman. Cognition, again, has its contractions and expansions. These two attributes are temporary while cognition itself is eternal. Kumārila holds cognition to be a pariṇāma (product) of Ātman. Though this product is temporary, still Ātman is eternal. Thus, we find in the Ātmavāda of the Śloka-Vārttika :

'अविनाशी स्वरूपेण पुरुषो या तु नाशिता ।
मात्राणां ... ... ॥

'This Puruṣa is of an undying nature. Death belongs to the organs of sense'.[2] According to Rāmānuja, Ātman is atomic in size; so, he cannot hold that cognition is a pariṇāma (product) of Ātman; for, an atom is incapable of forming a product. As regards the Jaina theory that Ātman is of the size of the body, we shall speak later on. In the Bhāṭṭa view, Ātman is omnipresent and is capable of forming a pariṇāma; but, still, the Bhāṭṭas conceive that Ātman is everlasting. On this point, the Vārttika says :

1. Nyāyaratnāvalī p. 13.
2. Ātmavāda, 147.

'स्यातामत्यन्तनाशेऽस्य कृतनाशाकृतागमौ ।
न त्ववस्थान्तरप्राप्तौ ।'[1]

'If Ātman has an absolute end, performances will go for nothing; and, things will occur which are not the results of past deeds. But, Ātman does not perish simply by undergoing changes'. It is not change but absolute destruction that makes a thing transitory. But, Ātman is not liable to absolute destruction. Hence, there is no objection to regarding it as eternal. If all are agreed that a thing should be treated as transient because of its changeableness, let it be so regarded. All that the Bhāṭṭas want to assert is that Ātman is not subject to destruction; and, that the transitoriness which is due to destruction should not be ascribed to Ātman. Thus, Kumārila says in the Ślokavārttika :

'नानित्यशब्दवाच्यत्वमात्मनो विनिवार्यते ।
विक्रियामात्रवाचित्वे न ह्युच्छेदोऽस्य तावता ॥'[2]

'If mere changeableness be the cause of transitoriness, Ātman may be called transitory. But, this does not by any means imply a destruction of it (Ātman)'. This śloka makes the position of the Bhāṭṭas clear by stating that even the eternal Ātman is subject to changes, such as cognition, etc. This view appears in the doctrines of the Śuddhādvaita, the Tāntrika and the Sāṁkhya-Pātañjala systems. According to the Śuddhādvaitins, God evolves himself into the form of the world; but, he is eternal all the same. The Tantra also propounds that Śakti evolves herself; but, it is still eternal. Similarly,

1. Ātmavāda, 23.
2. Op. cit., 22.

the Sāṁkhya-Pātañjala and the Pāśupata systems hold that Prakṛti, though eternal, is evolved into the shape of the world. The arguments advanced on this subject by all the these systems are the same as those of the Bhāṭṭa. Even the Vaiśeṣikas and the Naiyāyikas admit that the eternal Ātman is the substratum of cognition which is transitory.

ĀTMAN IS OMNIPRESENT

The followers of Rāmānuja preach that Ātman is of the size of an atom. This view of theirs is deduced from the following passage of the Śruti : 'आराग्रमात्रो ह्यवरोऽपि दृष्टः'. 'The most excellent being is perceived as the point of an awl'. If Ātman be atomic in size, how can it feel pleasure, pain, etc. all over the body ? The answer would be that it can do so through the medium of jñāna which is a property of its own and which is capable of contraction and expansion. They cite the example of a lamp to explain this view. The flame of a lamp is a pretty little thing; but, it can illumine many things by means of its rays of light which are capable of expansion. So, there is no harm in assuming that Ātman is atomic in size. But, it should be discussed here whether this jñāna which is an attribute of Ātman is different from Ātman or is identical with it. If it be regarded as different, an experience of pleasure or pain at a certain part of the body will belong to jñāna and not to Ātman; and so, Ātman will not be able to feel pleasure or pain. Jñāna cannot serve as a medium (vyāpāra) of Ātman, for, ia that case, it must be supposed that it is caused by

Ātman[1], as the light of a flame which illumines various articles is itself caused by the flame. But, Rāmānuja regards jñāna as eternal and independent and not as a product; and so, he cannot successfully propound that jñāna is a medium of Ātman. If it now be supposed that jñāna is not different from Ātman, another difficulty will arise. Jñāna, according to them, has contractions and expansions. If cognition be regarded as identical with Ātman, these expansions and contractions will be attributed to Ātman itself. But, Ātman, which is an atom according to them, is incapable of expanding or contracting. To effect expansions and contractions a large number of particles is necessary. But, as an atom has no particles, it cannot expand or contract. Hence, the Jainas propound that Ātman is of the size of the body. They hold that the subtle form of Ātman is capable of expansion and contraction. When it is born as an ant it will expand itself as much as is necessary to cover the body of the ant; and, when, in another birth, it is born as an elephant, it will expand itself more so as to cover the big body of the elephant. The advantage of this theory is that, according to it, we can explain how pleasure or pain, generated in any part of the body, is felt by Ātman. But, anything which is made up of component parts, as a jar or a piece of cloth, is liable to destruction. In assuming that Ātman is of the size of the body, which expands and contracts, the Jainas cannot but admit that Ātman consists of parts. So, it is not possible for them to support the eternal existence

1. तज्जन्यत्वे सति तज्जन्यजनकत्वं व्यापारत्वम् ।

of Ātman. It is for this reason that in the sūtra 'एवञ्च आत्माकार्त्स्न्यम्'.[1] of the Uttara-Mīmāṁsa, the Advaitins establish the omnipresence of Ātman by refuting the Jaina theory that Ātman is of the size of the body. But, Rāmānuja utilizes this sūtra for propounding his theory of the atomic size of Ātman by refuting the Jaina theory. We do not understand why Rāmānuja assails the Jaina theory at all. His objection is that, according to the Jaina theory, Ātman is capable of expansion and contraction, and, hence, it cannot be eternal. When he admits that cognition, which is an attribute of Ātman and which is capable of expansion and contraction, is eternal, why can he not hold that Ātman (of the Jainas) which is capable of contraction and expansion is, eternal? So, the theory of Rāmānuja is practically no improvement upon the Jaina theory.[2]

Hence, the Bhāṭṭas assume that Ātman is omnipresent. Although Ātman is all-pervading and individuals are numerous, still, what is known by one person is not known by another, because there is a particular demarcation of each individual which is due to different merits, demerits, etc. The passage, 'आकाशवत् सर्वगतश्च नित्यः,' 'Ātman is all-pervading and eternal like ether,' of the Śruti recognises the omnipresence as well as the eternal existence of Ātman. That text of the Śruti which describes Ātman as being of the size of the point of an awl does not really refer to Ātman itself.

1. II. ii. 34.

2. This matter has been fully discussed by Umāmaheśvara Śāstri in his Virodha-virodhinī.

When we say that a man is dead, we do not mean that this Ātman is dead, but the physique of the man, which is a disguise (उपाधि) of his Ātman, is dead. Similarly, in this passage, the word 'avara' does not mean Ātman itself, but it means 'manas' which is also a disguise of Ātman. We do not find any necessity for imagining an atomic size of Ātman. If it is done with a view to distinguishing Ātman from Brahman, we must say that it is unnecessary; for, the Naiyāyikas have successfully proved the omnipresence of Ātman without ever holding that it is identical with Brahman.

We ought to point out here that this theory of the omnipresence of Ātman does not rest upon the Sūtras of Jaimini but upon the Vedānta-Sūtras. We have seen above what different deductions Śaṅkara and Rāmānuja have made from the sūtra 'एवञ्च आत्माकार्त्स्न्यम्'. It is not proper to expatiate upon it here; but, it will suffice to notice that Kumārila has not accepted the theory of the atomic size of Ātman. He describes Ātman as 'सर्वगतः पुमान्'–an all-pervading entity; and, he also declares that the knowledge of Ātman will be developed by the study of the Vedānta. Hence, it is clear that the theory of omnipresence is in his opinion the proper deduction from the Vedānta-Sūtras.

ĀTMAN AS THE AGENT AND THE ENJOYER

In the Sāṁkhya-Pātañjala doctrine, Ātman is described only as the enjoyer. But, one who does not do anything cannot produce any result and cannot, consequently, enjoy anything. So, those who admit that Ātman is the enjoyer must admit also that it is a doer or an agent.

We have shown before that the difference between the views of the Bhāṭṭas and the Naiyāyikas is that while the former regard Ātman as consciousness, the latter hold that it is not so. If we accept the view of the Naiyāyikas as correct, we shall not be able to explain such texts of the Śruti as 'विज्ञानं यज्ञं तनुते' 'Consciousness performs sacrifices,' etc., where the word vijñāna clearly denotes Ātman. It is used here in the nominative case; and, so, it is the agent of the performance. So, the view of the Bhāṭṭas is quite consistent with this and other similar Śruti texts.

We may, also, briefly indicate here some other points of difference which exist between the views of the Bhāṭṭa and other systems. The Bhāṭṭas differ from the Cārvākas in holding the view that Ātman is eternal; from the Pāśupatas and Jainas in holding that Ātman is omnipresent; from the Bauddhas in maitaining the doctrine of the permanent consciousness of Ātman; and from the Sāṁkhya-Pātañjalas in holding that Ātman is a doer as well as an enjoyer.

There is really no difference of opinion between the Mīmāṁsakas and the Advaitins regarding these attributes. But, though both Bhaṭṭa and Prabhākara approve of the view of the Advaitins, they do not like to introduce that view into the Karma-Mīmāṁsā. We have said this once before. We cite below, once again, certain passages to emphasise the point under consideration :

'प्रमातृरूपता च ज्ञानस्यानाशङ्कनीयैव, अनाशङ्कितत्वाद् युक्तश्चेदं नाशङ्कितं कर्मप्रवणत्वात् ।'[1]

1. Bṛhatī, p. 254

'यदुक्तमहङ्कारममकाराद्यनात्मन्यात्माभिमानाविति मृदितकषायाणामेवैतत् कथनीयं न कर्मसङ्गिनामित्युपलभ्यते। आह च भगवान् द्वैपायनो 'न बुद्धिभेदं जनयेदज्ञानां कर्मसङ्गिनामिति रहस्याधिकारे।'[1]

'यदि परं ब्रह्मविदामेव निश्चयो यदुपलभ्यते तदसत्यम्। यन्नोपलभ्यते तत् तत्त्वमिति, नमस्तेभ्यः। विदुषि नोत्तरं वाच्यम्।'[2]

'इत्याह नास्तिक्यनिराकरिष्णुरात्मास्तितां भाष्यकृदत्र युक्त्या।
दृढत्वमेतद्विषयश्च बोधः प्रयाति वेदान्तनिषेवणेन॥'[3]

Now, it may be asked that if Kumārila and other Mīmāṁsakas approve of the view of the Advaitins, why do we find such passages as एतेनोपनिषदो व्याख्याताः' etc., in the Tantravārttika and other works which indicate that the Upaniṣad texts are arthavādas ?

The sentence 'एतेनोपनिषदो व्याख्याताः' of the Vārttika is explained in the Nyāyasudhā in the following way :

'एतच्च संसारिरूपात्मप्रतिपादनाभिप्रायम्। असंसारिरूपसगुणनिर्गुणात्मज्ञानस्याभ्युदयनिःश्रेयसार्थतया साधु शब्दाधिकरणे वक्ष्यमाणत्वात्, सिद्धार्थप्रतिपादनपराणामप्युपनिषदामुपासनाविधिशेषतया चोदनाशब्देनोपादानसम्भवाच्चोदनासूत्रप्रतिज्ञातप्रामाण्यसाधनं सङ्गतम्।'[4]

'This statement is made with reference to those Upaniṣad texts only which describe the Saṁsārī-Ātman (agent and enjoyer) and not to those texts which speak of an Asaṁsārī (released) Ātman, because the knowledge of the Asaṁsārī-Ātman, Saguṇa-Ātman (immanent)

1. Bṛhatī, p. 256
2. Op. cit., p. 239
3. Ātmavāda p. 148
4. Nyāyasudhā p. 25 (Ben. Ed.).

Brahman or Nirguṇa (Transcendental) Brahman as giving rise to the attainment of heavenly bliss or final beatitude, will be clearly described (by Kumārila) in the Śabdādhikaraṇa. Even the Upaniṣad texts which are statements of fact are supplements to the injunction for worship and, so, they may be included under 'codanā'. Hence, it is reasonable to hold that they possess that authoritativeness which is enunciated in the Codanā-sūtra'.

In the Śabdādhikaraṇa which is referred to in the Nyāyasudhā, Kumārila says : 'अप्रकरणगतत्वेनानैकान्तिकक्रतुसम्बन्धासम्बन्धाच्च नाञ्जनखादिरसुवर्णवाक्यादिफलश्रुतिवदर्थवादत्वम्'[1]. 'These (Upaniṣad) texts are not found in the context of any sacrificial injunction, nor do they describe things which are restricted exclusively to sacrifices; and, so, they are not to be treated as arthavādas like the phala-śruti passages regarding añjana, khādira, gold, etc. Arthavādas are generally found in the context of some sacrificial injunctions, and they eulogise or condemn something which is to be used or rejected in a sacrifice. The Upaniṣad texts are not of this kind. There are also other arthavādas which are not found in the context of any particular injunction; but, they praise or condemn something whose only use lies in sacrifices, such as 'juhu', etc,; and, on that account, they are connected with all sacrificial injunctions. But, the Asaṁsārī-Ātman, Saguṇa-Brahman or Nirguṇa-Brahman has nothing to do with any sacrifice. Hence, the Upaniṣad texts which speak of this Asaṁsārī-Ātman, Saguṇa-Brahman or Nirguṇa-Brahman, are not arthavādas.

1. Tantravārttikā, p. 241

The above explanation of the Nyāyasudhā makes it clear that Kumārila is not of the opinion that all Upaniṣad texts are arthavādas, and that he does not assail the view of the Advaitins, who regard Ātman as asaṁsāri (released). So, it is not proper to suppose that Kumārila disregards the Monistic Vedānta because he has said that Upaniṣad texts are arthavādas. Pārthasārathi Miśra also favours this view. In the Śāstradīpikā we find the following :

'यानि पुनरितिकर्तव्यताविशेषयुक्तानि उपासनात्मकानि ज्ञानानि विधीयन्ते तेषां क्रतौ दृष्टोपयोगाभावाददृष्टफलत्वम्। अदृष्टञ्च फलं वाक्यशेषाद् द्विविधम्, अभ्युदयरूपं निःश्रेयसरूपञ्च'[1]

'The precepts relating to worship which are laid down together with the rules of procedure, are found to be of no use to the sacrifices; and, therefore, they are supposed to produce unseen merits. From the remaining portion of the sentence we learn that an unseen result is of two kinds—attainment of heavenly bliss and final beatitude......'. There is only this difference between the opinion of Pārthasārathi and the author of the Nyāyasudhā that the former, by asserting that the knowledge relating only to worship produces the attainment of heavenly bliss, etc., concludes that Kumārila recognises the value of that Darśana only which deals with Saguṇā-upāsanā, while the latter indicates that Kumārila recognises the worth of Advaita Darśana also. But, there is no difference of opinion regarding the point that all Upaniṣad texts are not arthavādas.

1. Śāstradīpikā, I. i. 5

The above-mentioned Darśana dealing with Saguṇa-worship is not, however, the same as the Rāmānuja, the Pāśupata or the Mādhva Darśana, for these Darśanas acknowledge the atomic view of Ātman; but, the Śāstradīpikā holds Ātman to be omnipresent.

From the above discussion, another point becomes clear. The authors of the Nyāyasudhā and the Śāstra-dīpikā are decidedly of the opinion that the Bhāṭṭas are theists and nothing but theists. We may suppose that the distinction between the Bhāṭṭas and other theists is that the former hold that upāsanā itself produces its proper fruit, whereas the latter preach that God awards the fruit due on an upāsanā. There is another fundamental distinction : while all other theists declare that liberation is achieved through jñāna, Kumārila holds that it is produced by jñāna and karman combined.

We see, however, that the position of the Vedānta Darśana will not be affected even if all the Upaniṣad texts are regarded as arthavādas. Kumārila admits that even the arthavādas serve as authorities for things which cannot be known from any other source or which are not opposed to anything ascertained by any other means of proof. It is for this reason that all the Mīmāṁsakas while explaining the sūtra, 'Liṅga-darśan-ācca' in the Śabdanityatvādhikaraṇa,[1] accept the arthavāda, **'वाचा विरूपनित्यया'**, as an authority for the conclusion that sound is eternal.

---

1. Jaimini-Sūtra I. i. 23

Moreover, the texts which establish the existence of an Asaṁsārī-Ātman may be construed as eulogising the Saṁsārī-Ātman, and may still be regarded as the authorities for proving the existence of the Asaṁsārī Ātman. The Upaniṣad texts speak of the Asaṁsārī-Ātman. When Kumārila notices an eulogy of the Saṁsārī-Ātman in them he does not mean to deny that these texts describe an Asaṁsārī-Ātman; but, he simply means that such texts aim at eulogising the Saṁsārī-Ātman. But, how can the Saṁsārī-Ātman be praised by the texts which describe the Asaṁsārī-Atman ? To this, the answer would be that Jaimini has laid down a principle that where there is an eulogy of one correlative (सम्बन्धी) it may be intended for the other correlative also. In the passage, 'Take out fire by means of vetasa and avaka twigs; water is cool,' though water is praised as cool, the praise is really intended for the twigs that grow in water. So, the texts which tell us that Ātman is asaṃsārī are meant really for praising Saṁsārī-Ātman.

Hence, the Uttara-Mīmāṁsā will not lose its status as an independent Darśana even if all Upaniṣad texts be regarded as mere arthavādas, nor will an ascertainment of the nature of Ātman which is fit for performing sacrifices be impossible. This is what is meant by Kumārila when he says in the arthavādādhikaraṇa that the Upaniṣad texts are arthavādas. He does neither intend to condemn the Vedānta Darśana nor does he want to establish that the saṁsārī-Ātman cannot possess the attributes of the Asaṁsārī-Ātman. The passage of the Tantravārttika in the

Śabdādhikaraṇa, which we have quoted above, bears this out.

At the time of studying the Pūrva-Mīmāṁsā, we come to know that Ātman acts and enjoys the fruits of its actions; but, that must not lead us to reject the other conception of Ātman, viz., that it is Asaṁsārī, which is also derived from the Śrūti, though it stands in the way of the performance of sacrifices. This is the view of Kumārila; and, the following verse of the Ślokavārttika shows that it is so :

'इत्याह नास्तिक्यनिराकरिष्णुरात्मास्तितां भाष्यकृदत्र युक्त्या ।
दृढत्वमेतद्विषयश्च बोधः प्रयाति वेदान्तनिषेवणेन ॥'[1]

Kumārila states here clearly that the knowledge about Ātman will be developed by studying the Vedānta (the Upaniṣads). The purport of this statement is that there are certain attributes of Ātman which cannot be conceived at the time of the performance of sacrifices but which can be conceived with the help of the Vedānta. Thus, it appears to be the view of Kumārila that the acceptance of the apparent meaning of the Upaniṣad texts which is prejudicial to the performance of sacrifices is not advisable. But, it should by no means be asserted that Kumārila deprecates the Vedānta Darśana, merely on the basis of his statement that the Upaniṣad texts are arthavādas.

This shows another point of difference between the views of the Bhāṭṭas and the Naiyāyikas. The Naiyāyikas hold that Ātman is an agent, while the

1. Ātmavāda, 148

Bhāṭṭas hint that this character of Ātman is imaginary, though they do not give any pronounced opinion. We must not forget that the Prābhākaras are also of the same opinion. We have already cited some passages from the Bṛhatī which are to this effect.

So, we do not find any difference between the views of the Mīmāṁsakas and the Advaitins so far as the practical aspect of the Advaita doctrines are concerned. The Advaitins admit that Ātman, though it is of the nature of consciousness, is to be treated as 'jaḍa' or 'covered', because it is not perceived by others. They admit the eternal existence and omnipresence of Ātman. They also recognise its character as an agent etc., for all practical purposes. It is for this reason that the Advaitins openly declare that the doctrine of the Bhāṭṭas holds good for all practical purposes, viz., 'व्यवहारे भाट्टनयः'.

II. GOD

We have noticed before that a doubt is always raised as to whether the existence of God as a creator is admitted in the Pūrva-Mīmāṁsā. This doubt is principally due to the fact that Jaimini has not discussed about God in any one of his sūtras. Mādhavācārya, while giving a summary of the doctrines of the Pūrva-Mīmāṁsā in his Sarva-darśana-saṁgraha has mentioned all such doctrines as the doctrine of the uncreated character of the Vedas etc., but, he has not introduced any discussion about God. This fact also goes to strengthen the above doubt. So, many persons are led to think that atheism has the sanction and support of Jaimini. But, if we make a thorough investigation, we shall arrive at quite a different conclusion.

It has been shown in the first chapter that the name of Jaimini, the author of the Pūrva-Mīmāṁsā-Sūtras, is mentioned in the Sūtras of the Uttara-Mīmāṁsā. In the sūtra, 'धर्मं जैमिनिरत एव',[1] Bādarāyaṇa indicates that Jaimini does not recognise God as one who is instrumental in bringing about the enjoyment of results; but, Bādarāyaṇa does not say that Jaimini denies the existence of God as the creator. In the third chapter of the Uttara-Mīmāṁsā-Sūtras, discussions are made only about sādhanā; and, it is not probable that a denial of creatorship would be introduced there. Such discussions are made in the second chapter of the sūtras; and, if Bādarāyaṇa thought that apūrva was the cause of the creation of the world according to Jaimini, he would certainly have spoken of that in that chapter. But, in the second chapter we find no such sūtra. This fact clearly shows that the differenee between Jaimini and Bādarāyaṇa is only with regard to 'phala-sādhanatva' and not with regard to 'kartṛtva'. Thus, we can conclude that theism has the approbation of Jaimini so far as he is represented by Bādarāyaṇa.

In the beginning of the fourth chapter of his Karma-Mīmāṁsā, Prof. Keith says : 'Though the Mīmāṁsā is

1. III. ii. 41

so deeply concerned with the sacrifice, it has no belief in the doctrine that the rewards of offerings are to be expected either from the deities to whom the offerings are directed to be made or from a God as creator or apportioner of reward or punishment'. The purport of this statement is, that the apportionment of fruits is the same thing as creation; and that, if God be not regarded as the apportioner of fruits, he should not be regarded as the creator. This statement follows from a consideration of a passage of Śaṅkarācārya's commentary on the sūtra 'पूर्वं तु बादरायणो हेतुव्यपदेशात्'[1]. That passage runs as follows :

'तदेव चेश्वरस्य फलहेतुत्वं यत् स्वकर्मानुरूपाः प्रजाः सृजति'

'God is regarded as the cause of fruits inasmuch as he creates beings in accordance with their own actions.' With reference to the same sūtra, the Bhāmatī observes :

'न हि जातु मृत्पिण्डदण्डादयः कुम्भकाराद्यनाधिष्ठिताः कुम्भाद्यारम्भाय प्रभवन्तो दृष्टाः……………तस्मादचेतनं कर्म वा अपूर्वं वा न चेतनानधिष्ठितं स्वतन्त्रं स्वकार्यं प्रवर्तितुमुत्सहते ।'

'Lumps of clay, etc., are never seen to produce pots, etc., unless they are handled by potters and others. So, an action or apūrva which is insentient cannot independently discharge its own functions unless it is guided by a sentient being……..' By citing the examples of 'lumps of clay etc.,' the author of the Bhāmatī makes it clear that apūrva cannot produce a fruit unless it is regulated by a sentient being. It is admitted on all hands that here the view of Jaimini

1. III. ii. 41

forms the pūrva-pakṣa and that of Bādarāyaṇa forms the uttara-pakṣa. In the latter it is established that God is the cause of fruits in so far as he creates things, i.e., God is the apportioner of fruits or the creator. From this it appears that in the pūrva-pakṣa view (doctrine of Jaimini) the production of fruits by apūrva is the same thing as the creation of the things of the world and that God has nothing to do with it. If this be not regarded as the view of Jaimini, there would remain no connection between the pūrva-pakṣa and the uttara-pakṣa. So, it seems that in the view of Jaimini there is a denial of God as the creator. Prof. Keith takes this to be so : 'The Vedānta sūtra (III. 2, 40[1]) expressly negates the idea that in Jaimini's view there was divine intervention in this regard, and the atheism of the Mīmāṁsā is regarded with such unanimity as to render it impossible to explain it away'.[2]

Now, from the sūtra, 'धर्मं जैमिनिरत एव' it is ascertained that in Jaimini's view, dharma is the cause of fruits. We ought to determine, in the first place, what the word 'fruit' means. From the following extract from Śaṅkarācārya's commentary on the sūtra 'फलमत उतपत्तेः'[3] We get a description of 'fruit' :

'स्यादेतत्। कर्म विनश्यत् स्वकाल एव स्वानुरूपं फलं जनयित्वा विनश्यति, तत् फलं कालान्तरितं कर्त्रा भोक्ष्यत इति तदपि न परिशुध्यति। प्राग् भोक्तृसम्बन्धात् फलत्वानुपपत्तेः। यत्कालं हि यत्सुखं दुःखं चात्मना भुज्यते तस्यैव लोके फलत्वं

1. Probably he mistakes it for 41.
2. Karma-mīmāṁsā, p. 61
3. III. i.i. 38

प्रसिद्धम्। न ह्यसम्बद्धस्यात्मना सुखस्य दुःखस्य वा फलत्वं प्रतियन्ति लौकिकाः।'

'It may be that an act, which is about to cease, ceases after producing its proper fruit in the course of its occurrence. The agent will enjoy that fruit at some other time. This view is not satisfactory, because a fruit is no fruit till it comes to be enjoyed by the agent. It is a well-known fact that pleasure or pain is called a fruit when it is experienced by a man and that a pleasure or a pain, so long as it is not connected with a man, is not regarded by people as a fruit'. Vācaspati Miśra explains this idea in his Bhāmatī :

न हि स्वर्ग आत्मानं लभतामित्यधिकारिणः कामयन्ते किन्तु भोग्योऽस्माकं भवत्विति। तेन यादृशमेभिः काम्यते तादृशस्य फलत्वमिति भोग्यमेव सत् फलमिति। न च तादृशं कर्मानन्तरमिति कथं फलं सदपि स्वरूपेण।'

'Agents do not desire that paradise should be enjoyed by itself; but, they desire that it should be an object of enjoyment to them. So, what they desire becomes a fruit when it comes to be enjoyed; and, it is not another act of that kind. How can it, therefore, be regarded as a fruit even when it exists (not enjoyed) ?' From this, it appears that karman is to be regarded as the cause of the fruit, if it brings about the enjoyment. And, surely Bādarāyaṇa understands this to be the view of Jaimini. The idea that, according to Jaimini, apūrva only is the cause of creation, is never conceived by Bādarāyaṇa. Had Bādarāyaṇa taken that to be the view of Jaimini, he would have refuted it in the second chapter where the views of the Sāṁkhya and other Darśanas have been refuted and not in the

Sādhanapāda. From the very fact that this matter has been dealt with in the Sādhanapāda, it appears that the dispute between Bādarāyaṇa and Jaimini is with regard to God as the apportioner of fruits, i.e., as a sādhana or means of bringing about the enjoyment of fruits, and not with regard to God as the creator of the things of the world as they exist, i.e., which are not in the state of being enjoyed. Śaṅkarācārya, too, while explaining the sūtra फलमत उपपत्तेः[1] says :

'तस्यैव ब्रह्मणो व्यवहारिक्यामीशित्रीशितव्यविभागावस्थायाम-यमन्यः स्वभावो वर्ण्यते ।'

'This another function is ascribed to the same Brahman, which prevails so long as the division into the controller and the controlled continues for practical purposes'. By this statement, Śaṅkarācārya brings forward the view that God is not only the controller but the apportioner of fruits also. Thus, it becomes clear that the sūtra 'धर्मं जैमिनिरत एव'[2] is meant to show nothing but the fact that, in the view of Jaimini, God is not the apportioner of fruits. In the same sūtra, Saṅkarācārya says :

'ईश्वरस्तु फलं ददातीत्यनुपपन्नम् । अविचित्रस्य कारणस्य विचित्रकार्यानुपपत्तेर्वैषम्यनैर्घृण्यप्रसङ्गात् ।'

'But, that God gives fruits is not reasonable, because an unmixed cause cannot produce effects of a mixed character and because partiality and cruelty will arise'. On this point, the Bhāmati says :

1. III. ii. 38

2. III. ii. 41

'कर्मभिर्वा शुभाशुभैः कार्यद्वैधोत्पादे रागादिमत्त्वप्रसङ्ग इत्याशयः ।'

'The purport of this is that. if good or bad acts produce consequences of two kinds, there will be a susceptibility'. If acts produce consequences through the pleasure or displeasure of God, God will be liable to partiality and cruelty. So, in order to keep God free from all susceptibilities, we must admit that acts produce consequences through apūrva, and not through the pleasure or displeasure of God. This is what is understood by the author of the Bhāmatī to be the view of Jaimini.

Here, we must notice that at the time of refuting the view of Jaimini, Śaṅkarācārya says that the apportioner of fruits and the creator are the same :

'तदेव च ईश्वरस्य फलदातृत्वं यत् स्वकर्मानुरूपाः प्रजाः सृजति ।'

From this, it becomes clear that God cannot be regarded as the creator unless he is taken to be the apportioner of fruits. Now, the sentence, यत् स्वकर्मानुरूपाः प्रजाः सृजति, contains the word यत् which indicates that the statement is an अनुवाद i.e., a repetition. An anuvāda is possible only in the case of a thing of which we have known already and not in the case of a thing of which we know nothing. But, if God were not regarded as the creator of the world in the doctrine of Jaimini, it would by no means be possible to mention that matter as an accepted fact at the time of referring to his doctrine. Jaimini and Bādarāyaṇa dispute only over the manner of clearing God of the charges of partiality and cruelty. Jaimini holds that God himself does not award rewards or punishments which come through apūrva; while Bādarāyaṇa holds that God himself awards rewards and punishments, but he is not guilty of any partiality or cruelty; for, he acts in accordance with the acts done by individuals. So, we see that there is no dispute regarding the creatorship of God at all.

There can not, therefore, arise any doubt regarding the existence of God in Jaimini's system. The mere fact that Jaimini denies an intervention on the part of God in the matter of the apportionment of fruits does not amount to a denial of the existence of God. In support of our conclusion, we quote here the opinion of Prof. Max Müller : 'Here, then, we see the real state of the case as between Jaimini and Bādarāyaṇa. Jaimini would not make the Lord responsible for the injustice that seems to prevail in this world and hence, reduced everything to cause and effect and saw in the inequalities of the world the natural result of the continued action of good or evil acts. This surely, was not atheism, rather it was an attempt to clear the Lord from those charges of cruelty or undue partiality which have so often been brought against him. It was but another attempt of justifying the wisdom of God, an ancient Theodicee, that, whatever we may think of it, certainly did not deserve the name of atheism.'[1]

After these discussions, we cannot but reject the sweeping statement of Prof. Keith which is as follows :

1. Six Systems, p. 277

'The atheism of the true Mīmāṁsā is regarded with such unanimity as to render it impossible to explain it away (as does Max Müller etc.).'[1]

There is a tradition also, which ascribes atheism to Jaimini. In the sūtra, धर्मं जैमिनिरत एव, the doctrine of Jaimini, as we have seen above, seems to be represented as establishing dharma as the cause of rewards and punishments to the exclusion of God. Most probably, the origin of the above tradition lies here. Again, while supporting the view that God is the cause of rewards and punishments in the sūtra, फलमत उपपत्तेः, Śaṅkarācārya has proposed two pūrvapakṣas. The first of them runs thus :

'स्यादेतत् । कर्म विनश्यत् स्वकाल एव स्वानुरूपं फलं जनयित्वा विनश्यति, तत् फलं कालान्तरितं कर्त्रा भोक्ष्यत इति ।'

'An act, which is about to cease, ceases after producing its proper fruit during the course of its occurrence. The agent will enjoy that fruit at some other time.' The second one is as follows: 'अथोच्येत, माभूत् कर्मानन्तरं फलोत्पादः, कर्मकार्यादपूर्वात्फलमुत्पत्स्यत इति'. 'If you contend that the fruit may not directly follow the act but that the act produces an apūrva which gives rise to the fruit etc....' We have discussed the first pūrva-pakṣa already and have shown that the cause (apportioner) and the creator are different (in the view of Jaimini). Consequently, though God is not regarded as the cause (apportioner) of the fruits, still it cannot be said that He is not the creator. But the second pūrva-pakṣa goes

1. Karma-Mīmāṃsā, p. 61

so far as to ascribe even the creation of the world to 'karman' which is insentient. The effect of making such an assumption is that God as a creator is ousted; and, atheism gains ground. It may seem probable that the second pūrva-pakṣa also has been framed in accordance with the view of Jaimini. From this also the notion may have arisen that Jaimini was an advocate of atheism.

But, we must notice here that there is no reason for supposing that the second pūrva-pakṣa is based on Jaimini's view. Had Bādarāyaṇa understood Jaimini's view to be atheistical he would have framed the sūtra, धर्मं जैमिनिरत एव in another way. In the view of Jaimini, as represented here, dharma is regarded as the cause of the fruits on the strength of the Śruti texts and not on account of the non-existence of God. Had Bādarāyaṇa known Jaimini to be an atheist he would certainly have framed this sūtra as, धर्मं जैमिनिरभावात् . But, he has not done so. From this we infer that the second pūrva-pakṣa does not represent the view of Jaimini. Even if we accept Bādarāyaṇa's opinion that the apportioner of fruits is the same as the creator, it might still be suggested that 'karman' (and not God) is both the maker and apportioner of fruits. This suggestion gives rise to the second pūrva-pakṣa. The second pūrva-pakṣa is, therefore, a mere suggestion, and not an independent pūrva-pakṣa such as is required to be refuted separately by the sūtra, फलमत उपपत्तेः . The first pūrva-pakṣa is the principal pūrva-pakṣa. It clearly states that the creator and the apportioner of fruits are different. So, we can safely conclude that, in the view of Jaimini, God is the creator, but that he is not the apportioner of fruits. There is, therefore, no basis for the notion that Jaimini's system is atheistical.

Next, we come to Kumārila and Prabhākara, the principal expounders of the system of Jaimini. Prof. Keith accuses them also of atheism : 'The full development of the doctrine (atheism) is, as usual, to be found in Prabhākara and Kumārila'[1] So, we must carefully examine if Kumārila and Prabhākara are really supporters of atheism.

The views of the Prābhākaras regarding God are summarised by Dr. Jha in the following words : Prābhākara denies a creator for the universe. Even though he admits that the universe is made of constituent parts, and, as such, it must have a beginning and an end in time, yet he finds no reason for believing that the universe, as a whole, had a beginning at any one point of time, or that it would all come to an end at any one point; hence, if the constituent factors of the universe have a beginning, they must have beginnings one after the other; in fact, this is what is actually found to be the case in everyday experience. Thus, then, if it were true that certain factors of the universe are brought into existence by an ultra-mundane supervisor of dharma-adharma, this could not be true for the entire universe as a whole. For instance, the bodies of all men and animals are found to be produced by the functioning of the parents, and not by a supervising agency; and this fact will enable us to infer the same with regard to the bodies of all animals, past and future also'.[2]

1. Karma-Mīmāṁsā, p. 61
2. Indian Thought, Vol. II, p. 269

Dr. Jha states next the views of Kumārila very briefly : 'Kumārila's views with regard to God are found in the Ślokavārttika, Saṁbandhākṣepaparihāra. He also denies the creation (śloka 47) and dissolution (68) of the universe as a whole (113); he bases his denial of the creator on the same grounds as that of the 'omniscient person' (47–59, 114-16).[1]'

We must point out, here, that this denial of God has been made by Kumārila, Śālikanātha or any body else in the chapter on Saṁbandhākṣepaparihāra only with a particular object, and that this is not an absolute denial. They have made this denial only to show that even God has no independent control over the Vedas as is held by the Nyāya-Vaiśeṣikas. They also apprehend that if they accepted the view of the Naiyāyikas that the existence of God as the creator is to be ascertained by inference and that the Vedas are not uncreated, it would not be possible to support the existence of God. The simile, **सर्वज्ञवत्**, which is used by Kumārila in the verse, **'सर्वज्ञवन्निषेध्या च स्रष्टुः सद्भावकल्पना,'** 'the assumption of the existence of the creator should be rejected like the omniscience of Buddha', is very significant. In Nyāya-ratnamālā, the passage is explained thus :

'यथा च बुद्धादेः सर्वज्ञत्वं पुरुषत्वाद्अस्मदादिवन् निषेध्यम्, एवं प्रजापतेरपि स्रष्टृत्वम् ।'

'As the omniscience of Buddha cannot be proved from such a statement as 'Buddha is omniscient' because he was a man like ourselves, so is the creatorship of Prajāpati, (the Lord of creation)'. The

1. Indian Thought, Vol. II, P. 262

commentator means hereby to say that the truth of this theory (Prajāpati's creatorship) cannot be proved by means of arguments. The further significance of this verse has been stated in the first chapter of this work.

While criticising the view of the Naiyāyikas, Kumārila has let fall hints which indicate his belief in the existence and creatorship of God. That refutation is very lucidly presented by Prof. Keith which runs as follows : 'The Nyāya-Vaiśeṣika, accepting the doctrine of atoms on the one hand and of the periodical creation and destruction of the world on the other, had found it necessary to introduce the conception of a creator, in order to secure in some measure a mode of bringing about the renewal and destruction of the combinations of the atoms and their connection with souls. But, Prabhākara and Kumārila alike deny absolutely the validity of the belief in the periodical creation and dissolution of all things; they accept a constant process of becoming and passing away; but, they find no ground for the systematisation of the process, so as to produce cycles of evolution and involution of souls. Experience, Prabhākara urges, shows us the bodies of all animals being produced by purely natural means; hence, we can argue to the facts of the past and the future, and need invoke no extraneous aid. Moreover, the whole conception of God supervising the merits and demerits of men, is idle. God cannot perceive merit and demerit by perception, since they are not perceptible, nor by the mind, which is confined to the body it occupies. Supervision, also, is impossible. Even if God had the necessary knowledge it must take the form either of contact, which is impossible, as merit and demerit being qualities are not subject to contact or inherence, and, further, a man's qualities can not inhere in God. If the argument is adduced of the analogy of the carpenter, it may be replied that on this basis the creator would have to be an embodied spirit, and no embodied spirit can affect such subtle things as the atom or merit and demerit. Nor, is it conceivable that atoms should themselves act under the will of God, for no parallel to such activity is known to us. And, if it were possible, it would follow from the eternity of the will of God that creation would be unceasing'.[1] There is not the slightest doubt that the last sentence of the above extract is a paraphrase of the following verse which is found at the end of the refutation of atomic theory in the Ślokavārttika : 'तस्मान्न परमाण्वादेरारम्भः स्यात् तदिच्छया'[2]. 'It is not possible, therefore, that atoms should act under the will of God'. Now, the statement that atoms do not act under the will of God, will have a significance only when it is admitted that Kumārila recognises the existence of God and his creatorship and not his will as the cause of creation.

Thus, according to Kumārila, God's will plays no part in the matter of creation. In the following verses of the Ślokavārttika Kumārila expounds this view :

ईश्वरेच्छा यदीष्येत सैव स्याल्लोककारणम् ।
ईश्वरेच्छावशित्वे च निष्फला कर्मचोदना ॥

1. Karma-Mīmāṃsā, p. 61
2. Op. cit., p. 62

न चानिमित्तया युक्तमुत्पत्तुं हीश्वरेच्छया।
यद् वा तस्या निमित्तं यत् तद् भूतानां भविष्यति ॥[1]

'If you want to introduce the will of God, that itself will be the cause of the world. Under the paramount will of God, karman will shrink into insignificance. It is not also reasonable that God's will arises without any cause. That (adṛṣṭa) which may be suggested as its cause may as well be the cause of the world'. So, we see that Kumārila simply asserts that the will of God has nothing to do with creation, but he denies neither his existence nor his creatorship.

Prof. Keith says again : 'If, again, it is alleged that the creation was for his amusement this contradicts the theory, that he is perfectly happy and would involve him in much wearisome toil'.[2] We should bear in mind that this statement is a reiteration of the fifty-sixth verse of the Saṁbandhākṣepaparihāra which is a refutation of the view of the Naiyāyikas only. But, this attack is not directed against the sūtra, **'लोकवत् तु लीला-कैवल्यम्'** '(This creation is) his mere play as (we find) in the ordinary worldly affairs', of the Uttara-Mīmāṁsā.[3] The very same view is expressed by the Naiyāyikās and the Vedāntins. But, Kumārila attacks the Naiyā-yikas and exempts the Vedāntins. This fact is very significant. The only difference between the two systems is that the former has tried to prove the existence of God by means of arguments and the latter has tried to derive the idea of God from the Śruti. There

1. Saṁbandhākṣepaparihāra, 72–3
2. Karma-Mīmāṁsā, p. 63
3. Vedānta Sūtra, II. i. 33

is no dispute that the Vedānta Sūtras are based on the Śruti. In his commentary on the second sūtra of the Uttara-Mīmāṁsā, Śaṅkarācārya has said, 'वेदान्त-कुसुमग्रथनार्थत्वात् सूत्राणाम्' 'the sūtras are meant for culling the Vedānta flowers (i.e. the fine conclusions of the Upaniṣads)'. The sūtras deal with the utterances of the Upaniṣads and do not involve themselves in mere argumentation. Now, the real attitude of the Mīmāṁsaka becomes clear. If anybody tries to prove the existence of God by means of arguments, the Mīmāṁsaka will advance counter-arguments to attack him; but, if anybody tries to derive the same thing from the uncreated Śruti, the Mīmāṁsaka will not raise any objection. He denies that God who is the result of human deliberations; but, he does not deny that God who is found in the uncreated Śruti. This is certainly not atheism.

It is said, that 'God is perfectly happy'; and, so, there is no reason as to why he should make the creation for the sake of amusement (līlā). But, if we assume that God makes the creation in accordance with the respective acts of individuals, we shall be in a position to say that the creation is not for his amusement. In fact, the Mīmāṁsaka has so assumed. Those who preach that the creation is for the amusement of God will bear the brunt of the above attack. But, the Mīmāṁsaka stands at a safe distance. He regards God as a supervisor or judge. Just as a supervisor or judge acts in accordance with fixed rules of law, so God administers in accordance with our 'karman.'

But, both Dr. Jha and Dr. Keith have said that no supervision on the part of God is possible. We have quoted before what Dr. Keith has said on this matter and we quote below a few lines from Dr. Jha's work : 'Nor is there any force in the Logician's arguments that our dharma-adharma must have a supervisor, a being possessed of intelligence higher than our own. Because the dharma-adharma of the body that is the product of these must always belong to the same intelligent being to whom the body belongs; any being, howsoever intelligent, can never have any knowledge of the dharma-adharma of any other being; hence, the ultra-mundane 'God' can have no knowledge of the dharma or adharma of the beings born as men, animals etc., and without such knowledge he could not exercise any intelligent control over them; 'God' could not perceive dharma by his senses, as dharma is absolutely imperceptible; nor could he perceive it by his mind alone, as the mind by itself cannot perceive things outside the body; and the dharma of all beings born in the world would always be outside the body occupied by the mind of the perceiving person, 'God'.

Then again it becomes necessary to examine the character of the 'supervision' that 'God' is said to exercise over dharma and adharma. This supervision cannot be of the nature of contact or conjunction, because dharma and adharma being qualities are not capable of conjunction, which is possible for substances only. Nor, could it be in the form of samavāya or inherence, as the dharma-adharma inhering in other souls could not inhere in God.'[1]

But, we do not think that this is the true view of the Mīmāṁsā. God's supervison consists in an investigation into dharma and adharma performed by the individuals. By these words, 'dharma' and 'adharma,' the Mīmāṁsaka does not mean 'apūrva', but simply the performance of sacrifices, etc. Such performances, when made by one person, can be seen by another. So, it cannot be said that God cannot perceive dharma and adharma by perception. If dharma and adharma do not mean apūrva, it becomes unnecessary to examine further the character of the supervision of God, as both Dr. Jha and Dr. Keith have done. God remembers the acts done by individuals and makes His creations in accordance with those acts. In his Bhāṭṭa-cintāmaṇi Gāgā Bhāṭṭa has given us the same conclusion. He states that such texts of the Śruti as, तदैक्षत, etc., point to the adṛṣṭa (of individuals). In the Upaniṣads, there are such texts, as 'तदैक्षत' 'He (God) considered, 'सोऽकामयत' 'He desired', etc. The purport of such texts is that God creates in accordance with the previous acts of individuals.[2]

We point out once more that all these arguments of Kumārila which have been reproduced by Dr. Jha and Dr. Keith were adduced by him for refuting the views of the Nyāya-Vaiśeṣikas only, and that he does not deny the creatorship of God.

---

1. Indian Thought, Vol. II, pp. 259-260
2. Bhāṭṭa-cintāmaṇi, Ben. ed. p. 36

This affords a solution of the problem of creation and dissolution. The Mīmāṁsakas never admit an original creation or a total dissolution taking place at one point of time; but, they hold that creation and dissolution are perpetually going on. On this point the conclusion of the Vārttika is as follows :

तस्मादद्यवदेवात्र सर्गप्रलयकल्पना ।
समस्तक्षयजन्मभ्यां न सिध्यत्यप्रमाणिका ॥[1]

'Hence, creation and dissolution take place as (they are taking place) to day : there is no authority to prove that the whole (world) is created or destroyed at one time'. But, Kumārila is ready to believe that God is the cause of such creation and dissolution if only it is taken for granted that the Vedas are uncreated. If the Vedas are regarded to be a creation of God, the difficulty will be that we shall not be able to accept as true all that is said there about God. So, we shall have to depend upon inference for ascertaining such facts. But. inference is not possible in such cases where no parallel examples are known from our experience. We cannot, therefore, obtain any correct knowledge of God by adopting this process. What Kumārila wants to propound is that this difficulty will not arise if the Vedas be eternal and independent, for then the statements will lie beyond all suspicion and, so, it will hardly require any verification.

It seems to be the principal infention of Kumārila in attacking the theories of Naiyāyikas, the Sāṁkhyas, the Bauddhas and others, to refute their view that the

1. Saṁbandhākṣepaparihāra, p. 113

Vedas are a composition. Had they not held so, Kumārila would not have attacked them, may be, he would have supported them. The following extract from the Tantravārttika will corroborate the truth of the statement :

'याश्चैताः प्रधानपुरुषेश्वरपरमाणुकारणादिप्रक्रियाः सृष्टिप्रलयादिरूपेण प्रतीतास्ताः सर्वा मन्त्रार्थवादज्ञानादेव दृश्यमानस्थूलसूक्ष्मद्रव्यप्रकृतिविकारभावदर्शनेन च द्रष्टव्याः। प्रयोजनञ्च स्वर्गयागाद्युत्पाद्योत्पादकविभागज्ञानम्। सर्गप्रलयोपवर्णनमपि दैवपुरुषकारप्रभावप्रविभागप्रदर्शनार्थम्। सर्वत्र हि तद्बलेन प्रवर्तते, तदुपरमे चोपरमतीति। विज्ञानमात्रक्षणभङ्गनैरात्म्यादिवादानामप्युपनिषत्प्रभवत्वं विषयेष्वात्यन्तिकं रागं निवर्तयितुमित्युपपन्नं सर्वेषां प्रामाण्यम्। सर्वत्र च यत्र कालान्तरफलत्वादिदानीमनुभवासम्भवस्तत्र श्रुतिमूलता।[1]

'The actions of the causes, Pradhāna, Puruṣa, Īśvara or atoms, which are known as the creation and the dissolution, are to be understood from the mantras and the arthavādas, as well as from an observation of the natural and decomposed conditions of visible objects, gross or fine. The object is to obtain knowledge of the distinction between the effect and the cause, such as heavenly bliss, sacrifice, etc., The description of creation and dissolution is also meant to distinguish the influence of 'daiva' from that of 'puruṣakāra'; 'daiva' is the motive power in all cases and all cease when that ceases. Even the Vijñānavāda, the Kṣaṇabhaṅgavāda, the Nairātmyavāda, etc., have their origin in the Upaniṣads, and their object is to check an

1. Tantravārttika, p. 81

excess of attachment to the objects of the senses, and, hence their authority is admitted. And, in all the cases where the effect takes place at a distant time and consequently is incapable of being ascertained at present, the Śruti is to be depended upon'.

Here, Kumārila clearly states his opinion that all the doctrines which occur in the Bauddha Darśanas, etc., have their origin in the Upaniṣads, and that for this reason they constitute an authority on dharma. By this opinion it is implied that if the Bauddhas and others recognised dharma as resting on the authority of the eternal Vedas, he would readily accept their decision. His denial of the existence of God is nothing but a protest against the doctrine of the Naiyāyikas who have worked out the existence of God independently of the Śruti. So, from such an act of denial, it must not be supposed that Kumārila is a supporter of atheism. It is true that he has not separately substantiated theism. But, it was not necessary for him to do so. To him who is an earnest believer in the Śruti, the existence of God is nothing less than a self-evident truth, and there is no reason why he should make a special attempt to establish it. Still it cannot be said that he is silent with regard to his real opinion, for he has avowed it in the passage:

'तस्मात् प्रागपि सर्वेऽमी स्रष्टुरासन् पदादयः ।

... ...

एवं ये युक्तिभिः प्राहुस्तेषां दुर्लभमुत्तरं ॥[1]

'All the words, etc., must have, therefore, existed before the creation. It is very difficult to find an

1. Saṁbandhākṣepaparihāra, 116-7

answer against those who hold this by force of arguments'. The author of the Nyāyaratnākara explains this passage as follows :

'एवं स्रष्टुर्वेदपूर्वत्वं साधयतां न किञ्चिदुत्तरं भवति, तेन सत्यपि सर्गे सुप्तप्रबुद्धन्यायेन अनादिरेष वेदव्यवहारः ॥'

'There is no answering those who urge in this way that the Vedas had existed before the Creator. So, even admitting that there was a creation, the Vedas may be regarded as eternal according to the supta-prabuddha-nyāya'. In the Śāstradīpikā this view is corroborated in the most unequivocal terms :

'नित्यत्वे हि वेदानामवसिते तत्प्रामाण्यबलेन ईश्वरस्यापरिच्छेद्यो महिमा सृष्टिप्रलयौ च सिध्येयुर्न वा। वेदांस्तु अनादृत्य दृष्टानुसारेण पर्वत, इवानुमानमत्यन्तालौकिकार्थे प्रवर्तयतामुपेक्षैव इत्युत्तरमित्युपरम्यते ।'[1]

'If the eternity of the Vedas be admitted, the unlimited greatness of God and creation and dissolution (by Him) may or may not be established. But, to them who, in disregard of the Vedas, make inferences regarding the most supernatural things on the basis of the knowledge derived from experience, as in the case of the mountain, we must assume an air of indifference—that is our answer, and no more.'

Again, all possible doubts regarding Kumārila's belief in the existence of God will be removed if we look at the benedictory verse of the Ślokavārttika where he makes reverence to God, and at the following statement made by himself in the Grahaikatvādhikaraṇa :

1. Śāstradīpikā, p. 331 (Ben. Ed.)

शब्दब्रह्मेति यच्चेदं शास्त्रं वेदाख्यमुच्यते ।
तदप्यधिष्ठितं सर्वमेकेन परमात्मना ॥[1]

'This Śāstra called the Veda, which is Brahman in the form of sounds is watched over by God alone.' This is corroborated by the author of the Mīmāṁsā-nyāyaprakāśa (a leading exponent of the Bhāṭṭa school) who says :

'यः कल्पः स कल्पपूर्वक इति न्यायेन संसारस्यानादित्वादीश्वरो गतकल्पीयं वेदं स्मृत्वा उपदिशति ।'[2]

'According to the theory that one kalpa is preceded invariably by another kalpa, the world (is regarded) as having no beginning. Hence, (we conclude that) God reproduces from his memory the Vedas of the last kalpa and teaches them'.

In the Prakaraṇa-pañcikā discussions have been made about these points just in the same spirit as in the Vārttika. There, too, the denial of the existence of God has been made only in connection with the refutation of the theory that the relation between words and their meanings is creational. We quote here the very first sentence of that chapter (Saṁbandhākṣepaparihāra) of the Prakaraṇa-pañcikā :

तत्र शब्दार्थसम्बन्धं पौरुषेयं प्रचक्षते ।
जगदीश्वरनिर्माणं वदन्तो वेदवादिनः ॥

'Those teachers of the Vedas who maintain that the world is a creation of God declare that the relation between words and their meanings is pauruṣeya, i.e.,

1. Tantravārttika, p. 719
2. Mīmāṁsā-nyāyaprakāśa, para 1

creational'. If it be admitted that God created the whole world, then it would be assumed that he created words and meanings, as well as the relations existing between them. But, the Prābhākara wants to refute the theory that the relation between a word and its meaning is a creation; and in order to carry out this refutation he denies in the first place that the world is a creation of God. The Naiyāyikas and the Vaiśeṣikas have held that in the beginning of creation, God established the connection between words and their meanings. This theory of theirs is attacked in the chapter on Saṁbandhākṣepaparihāra of the Prakaraṇapañcikā just in the same manner as in the Vārttika. So, in the Prābhākara view, too, there would be no bar to admitting the existence of God if it only be assumed that the relation between words and their meanings is without any beginning.

Thus, it becomes clear that there is no difference between the Bhāṭṭa and the Prābhākara views regarding the existence of God, etc. The paramāṇu-vāda has been exploded by both these schools; but, they have not denied the existence of God. So, we do not find any truth in the statement of Dr. Keith, that the full development of Jaimini's atheistic doctrine is found in Prabhākara and Kumārila.

In the writings of some Indian commentators, too, we find that the Mīmāṁsakas have been represented as denying the existence of God. In the Siddhāntabindu, the following passage is found:

'नास्ति सर्वज्ञत्वाद्युपेतं ब्रह्म। आम्नायस्य क्रियार्थत्वेन तत्र तात्पर्याभावात्। किन्तु वाग्धेन्वादिवत् सर्वज्ञत्वादिदृष्ट्या

जगत्कारणं परमाण्वादि जीवो वा उपास्य इति मीमांसकाः ।[1]

'The Mīmāṁsakas say that there is no God endowed with omniscience, etc. Because the Vedas, which exist for sacrificial purposes, have nothing to do with him. But, as speech is likened to a cow, so either atoms, etc., or Ātman, may be regarded as endowed with omniscience, etc., and worshipped'. This passage has been thus explained in the Nyāyaratnāvalī:

'तथा च यतो वा इत्यादिश्रुतेः, यतः परमाण्वदृष्टादेर्जीवाद् वा, जगदुत्पत्त्यादिकं तत्सम्बद्धत्वादिदृष्ट्या उपासीत इत्यर्थं इति भावः ।'

'Again, owing to such texts as, यतो वा etc., the word यतः means the atoms, adṛṣṭa or Ātman, from which creation etc., of this world takes place. The purport is that it is to be regarded as endowed with omniscience, etc., and worshipped'.

But, these Mīmāṁsakas can by no means be identified with Kumārila and his followers; because, we know that Kumārila has clearly refuted the theory of atomic creation, has recognised by adopting अभिहितान्वयवाद्[2] the authoritativeness of such Vedic texts as deal with existing things, has admitted the existence of God on the authority of the uncreated Vedas and has recognised God as an object of worship.[3] We need not make any separate remark regarding the view of the Prābhākaras. In this view, also, the rule that Vedic texts exist for enjoining performances based on the sūtra, आम्नायस्य क्रियार्थत्वात्, etc.[4], will not be violated,

1. Siddhāntabindu p. 155
2. Op. cit. p. 80
3. Op. cit. p. 126
4. Jaimini-Sūtra I. ii. 1

if God is regarded as the object of the injunction of worship; for, the injunction of worship is also an injunction. We have said before that no particular view regarding God is found in the Bṛhatī or any other work of the Prābhākaras and that it is the same view as has been accepted by Kumārila that is found in the Prakaraṇa-pañcikā etc. Kumārila clearly avows Seśvaravāda in the Śabdādhikaraṇā by stating that both sacrifice and worship are necessary for effecting liberation. Still, the refutation of the inferential existence of God which is made by Kumārila at great length is the cause of the above remarks that we find in the Siddhāntabindu and other works.

THE BODY OF GOD

Now, when the Mīmāṁsakas admit the existence of God as the creator, they ought also to admit that God possesses a body; for, creation would never be possible without a body. But, Kumārila, while refuting the doctrine of atoms, shows by arguments that the existence of a body of God cannot be proved. His view is briefly stated by Dr. Keith in the following lines: 'He (Kumārila) ridicules the idea of the existence of Prajāpati before the creation of matter; without a body, how would he feel desire ? If he possessed a body, then matter must have existed before his creative activity and there is no reason to deny then the existence of other bodies.'[1]

But, here also, we must not forget that Kumārila denies the existence of such eternal body of the crea-

1. Karma-Mīmāṁsā, p. 61

tor as is proposed by the Naiyāyikas. The Naiyāyikas derive the idea of God by inference, which, however intelligent it may be, must necessarily depend upon human experience. But, men have never come across any eternal body anywhere. Hence, Kumārila says that we cannot ascertain an eternal body of God by inference. But, if the Vedas be supposed to be uncreated, and if the idea of God is derived from such Vedas, then Kumārila would not raise his voice against the existence of any kind of body of God which may be described there. He does actually describe God as having some sort of body in the benedictory verse of the Ślokavārttika.

We should consider one thing more in this connection. There are texts of the Śruti such as, वज्रहस्तः पुरन्दरः etc., which indicate that gods also have bodies. Why have then the Mīmāṁsakas held in the Devatādhikaraṇa[1] that gods do not possess physical forms? Here, in the first place, we should point out that this denial of the existence of physical forms is not the intention of the Mīmāṁsakas. The fourth sūtra of the Devatādhikaraṇa is worded thus:

अपि वा शब्दपूर्वत्वाद् यज्ञकर्म प्रधानं स्याद् गुणत्वे देवताश्रुतिः ।

'Or, the performance of sacrifices is the prominent element, because it follows directly from the words of the Vedas, and the deities have a minor position.' By this sūtra, Jaimini only lays down that the deities

1. Jaimini-sūtras: IX. i. 6-10

serve as subordinate elements in sacrifices; but, he does not say a word indicating the non-existence of their physical forms. So, we ought to inquire as to why this negation has been made by the Mīmāṁsakas in this sūtra.

In the Uttara Mīmāṁsā, there is a sūtra :

विरोधः कर्मणीति चेन्नानेकप्रतिपत्तेर्दर्शनात् ।[1]

'(If you argue that) there would be a contradiction so far as sacrifices are concerned; no—because, it is found (in the Śruti and the Smṛti) that one deity can assume many forms.' In the first part of this sūtra, the non-existence of physical forms of gods is suggested by Śaṅkarācārya and others under the apprehension that it would not be possible for gods who are an 'aṅga' of the sacrifice to complete the sacrifice by appearing in their actual physical forms. The idea that gods are an 'aṅga' of the sacrifice is borrowed from the Sūtras of Jaimini and from this it may have been presumed that the idea of the non-existence of the physical forms of gods also comes from Jaimini. By the last portion of the sūtra, 'अनेकप्रतिपत्तेर्दर्शनात्' it is established that the physical forms of gods are no bar to their serving in sacrifices. But, this conclusion of the Uttara Mīmāṁsā must not lead us to suppose that, in the view of the Pūrva Mīmāṁsā, gods have no physical forms. A consideration of the sūtra, 'मध्वादिष्वसम्भवादनधिकारं जैमिनिः'[2] of the Uttara Mīmāṁsā will corroborate the view that Jaimini does

1. Vedānta-sūtra I. iii. 27
2. Op. cit. I. iii. 31

not deny the existence of the physical forms of gods. This sūtra tells us that, in the view of Jaimini, gods are not entitled to study the brahma-vidyā, because they are not entitled to study the madhu-vidyā, etc., and not because they have no bodies. Had Jaimini contemplated that gods had no bodies, it would have been unnecessary to frame a pūrva-pakṣa, as it is not possible for the bodiless to undertake a study. But, a pūrva-pakṣa has been framed to represent his view which rests on a quite different ground altogether. Does not this fact make it clear that Jaimini did not deny the existence of the physical forms of gods ?

In the Śāstradīpikā also, Pārthasārthi Miśra has propounded, in the passage 'सत्यपि विग्रहे'[1] that gods serve in sacrifices, even after assuming that they possess physical forms. So, Pārthsārthi has solved the difficulty that was raised in the Devatādhikaraṇa. Still, as a matter of fact, elaborate discussions are found in many treatises of the Mimāṁsā which aim at denying the existence of the bodies of gods. What may be the reason of making this attempt ?

There is a doctrine of the Mīmāṁsakas that the letters of mantras are unalterable. If a single syllable is omitted or transposed, or if in the place of a particular word any synonym of it is used, the mantra will be defective and will not produce the desired effect. Hence, it is necessary that a mantra should be correctly pronounced. The sacrificer and priests

1. Śāstradīpikā, p. 580

are not required to see that gods are present at the time of the performance; but, they should only take care that they commit no mistake in uttering the mantras. They have nothing to do with gods as actual persons but they have only to deal with their names. Hence, arises the belief that gods exist in names; and, the Mīmāṁsakas have arrived at the conclusion that gods are identical with their respective names. In order to arrive at this conclusion, they have adduced various arguments to show the difficulties lying in the way of admitting the existence of the bodies of gods. Their main object is not to deny the existencc of the bodies of gods but to assert that it is the names of gods that are of all importance to us. Had it been the objeet of the Mīmāṁsakas to establish the view that gods are nothing but names, they would not have propounded in the Stotra-śāstrādhikaraṇa[1] that the stotras are meant not to .mention gods but to describe the qualities that are to be found in them. It would be absurd to hold that the qualities that are praised in such mantras, as, अभि त्वा शूर नोनुमः, etc., belong to gods who are nothing but sounds. Hence, we must come to the conclusion that in the view of the Pūrva Mīmāṁsā, gods are not absolutely identified with their names, The doctrine, that gods are names, is propounded simply to arouse an excessive feeling of reverence towards the Vedic mantras and the names of gods that are found in those mantras; but, truly speaking, no such identity exists. So, we do not think that there

1, II. i. 5

will be any opposition, if we state that, in the true view of the Mīmāṁsakas, gods are regarded as corporeal beings. The same conclusion has been arrived at in the Nyāya-mayūkha-mālikā, as well as in the Seśvara-mīmāṁsā Darśana.

GOD AS AN OBJECT OF WORSHIP

Like other theistic systems of Indian philosophy, the Pūrva Mīmāṁsā also preaches that God is an object of worship. We have already seen that in the Śabdādhikaraṇa, Kumārila has decided that the worship etc., of the Saguṇa God is also conducive to the attainment of heavenly bliss or salvation. We have also seen that this view is supported in the Nyāya-sudhā and the Śāstradīpikā. Again, in the very beginning of the Ślokavārttika Kumārila eulogises Śiva :

'विशुद्धज्ञानदेहाय त्रिवेदीदिव्यचक्षुषे ।
श्रेयःप्राप्तिनिमित्ताय नमः सोमार्धधारिणे ॥'

'Reverence to him whose body is made of pure knowledge, whose divine eyes are the three Vedas, who is the cause of the attainment of bliss, and who wears a digit of the moon.' This verse shows that Kumārila supports Seśvaravāda. Were he not in favour of Seśvaravāda, in would be anything but relevant. An attempt has actually been made in the Nyāyaratnākara to interpret the verse in another way:' It is the sacrifice to which the reverence is made here. The sacrifice requires correct knowledge for its performance, is made known by the Vedas, contains cups and pots of soma-juice and is the cause of the attainment of heavenly bliss, etc.' But, the commentator has not omitted to give the purport of the other interpretation also, which is as follows :

'श्लोकवार्त्तिकमारिप्सुस्तस्याविघ्नसमाप्तये ।
विश्वेश्वरं महादेवं स्तुतिपूर्वं नमस्यति ॥'

'Desiring to begin the Ślokavārttika, he bows to Mahādeva, the lord of the universe with the object of reaching the end safely'.

God is described here, as the cause of the attainment of bliss. How can this statement be consistent with the view of the Mīmāṁsakas who never admit that God's favour is in any way instrumental in producing bliss ?

There is, however, only one possible way of making the passage, श्रेयःप्राप्तिनिमित्ताय, consistent, and that is as follows : God is to be regarded as the general cause of bliss and not as its particular or special cause. By 'the general cause' we mean that he becomes the cause of all enjoyments only by creating necessary things. We have discussed this point fully before. An act of namaskāra (reverence) will bring a safe termination by generating an apūrva. If we take the above expression in this sense the question of God's favour will not arise and consequently there will be no difficulty.

We should notice here the peculiarities of the epithets of God that are found in the above verse. From the expression, 'त्रिवेदीदिव्यचक्षुषे', 'the three Vedas are His divine eyes', we learn that in all His activities God depends upon the knowledge derived from the Veda. So, in creating the world, God had recourse to the same resource. Hence, it is implied that the Veda could not be a creation of God. The other epithet, 'सोमार्धधारिणे', 'He who wears a digit of the moon', shows that He has a body. That this body is not made of the usual stuff is indicated by the first epithet, 'विशुद्धज्ञानदेहाय', 'His body consists of pure knowledge.' This epithet is apparently meant to denote that His body is composed of extraordinary elements; but, it has also a further significance. Jñāna is opposed to avidyā or nescience; and, it is implied, therefore, that God's person is beyond the influence of nescience. So, we get here an inkling of the doctrine of the Advaitins who hold that God is Nirguṇa (free from qualities) and is of the form of pure consciousness.

In this connection, it is necessary to point out that the following remark of Dr. Keith does not touch the Advaitins : 'Kumārila, however, does not content himself with refuting the Nyāya-Vaiśeṣika doctrine; attacks equally the Vedānta on the simple ground that if the absolute is, as it is asserted to be, absolutely pure, the world itself should be absolutely pure. Moreover, there could he no creation for nescience is impossible in such an absolute. If, however, we assume thet some other can start nescience to activity, the unity of the absolute disappears. Again, if nescience is natural, it is impossible to remove it; for, that could be accomplished only by knowledge of the self, which on the theory of the natural character of nescience, is out of the question.'[1] This statement is nothing but a reiteration of the verses :

---

1. Karma-Mīmāṁsā pp. 63–4.

'पुरुषस्य तु शुद्धस्य नाशुद्धा विकृतिर्भवेत् ।
... ... ॥'[1]

Here the word, puruṣa, does not mean Īśvara, for we find in the following passage of the Tantravārttika that the two words, 'ईश्वर' and 'पुरुष', have been used by Kumārila, side by side in the same sentence, 'प्रधानपुरुषेश्वरपरमाणुकारणादिप्रक्रिया...'[2]. This leaves no doubt that Kumārila uses the two words in different senses. Here, the word 'puruṣa' does not mean 'Nirguṇa Brahman' of the Advaita philosophy; for, the Advaitins have neither used it anywhere to denote Nirguṇa Brahman, nor do they admit that Nirguṇa Brahman subjects itself to evolution. The theory of the Advaitins is that the world is a vivarta (illusion) of Brahman. Under these circumstances it cannot be said that the passages, पुरुषस्य ..., are meant to refute the doctrine of the Advaitins. The author of the Śāstradīpikā also interprets the above verses, as refuting the Advaita doctrine. But, if any such Advaita doctrine ever existed, we must say that it is now lost to us. We do not know what that doctrine is, which he supports in the passages, 'केचित् तु औपनिषदाः...'.[3] It is true that in the sūtra, भोक्त्रापत्तेरविभागश्चेत् स्याल्लोकवत्[4] of the Vedānta, it is propounded that the world is an evolution of Brahman. But, this theory is a prima facie one and holds good for practical purposes only. Saṅkarācārya has shown in his commentary on the very next sūtra, तदनन्यत्वमारम्भण-

1. Sambandhākṣepaparihāra 82–7
2. Tantravārttika, p. 81
3. Śāstradīpikā p. 316
4. II. i. 13

शब्दादिभ्यः[1] that the vivarta-vāda is the real and proper theory of the Vedānta. On a consideration of all these points, we are able to say this at least that the view stated above by Dr. Keith, has nothing to do with the Advaita doctrine as propounded by Śaṅkara. So, the suggestion that the said benedictory verse of Kumārila indicates an inclination toward the Advaita doctrine stands unchallenged.

Again, in his commentary on the samanvaya-sūtra[2] Śaṅkarācārya makes a clear representation of the view of the Mīmāṁsakas regarding the purport of such Upaniṣad texts as describe Brahman in the paragraph beginning with the words : 'अत्रापरे प्रत्यवतिष्ठन्ते'. There he sets forth that the Mīmāṁsakas have construed the Vedānta texts as representing God as an object of worship :

'कार्यविधिप्रयुक्तस्यैव ब्रह्मणः प्रतिपाद्यमानत्वात् । आत्मा वा अरे द्रष्टव्यः, य आत्मा अपहतपाप्मा सोऽन्वेष्टव्यः स विजिज्ञासितव्यः, आत्मेत्येव उपासीत, आत्मानमेव लोकमुपासीत, ब्रह्म वेद ब्रह्मैव भवति, इत्यादिषु हि विधानेषु सत्सु, कोऽसावात्मा किं ब्रह्म इत्याकाङ्क्षायां तत्स्वरूपसमर्पणेन सर्वे वेदान्ता उपयुक्ताः, नित्यः सर्वज्ञः सर्वगतो नित्यतृप्तो नित्यशुद्धबुद्धमुक्तस्वभावो विज्ञानमानन्दं किं ब्रह्म इत्येवमादयः । तदुपासनाच्च शास्त्रदृष्टोऽदृष्टो मोक्षः फलं भविष्यति । कर्तव्यविध्यननुप्रवेशे वस्तुमात्रकथने हानोपादानासम्भवात् ।'

As a deity is an aṅga of a sacrifice so God is an aṅga of worship. Now, Śaṅkara would never have made such a representation if he knew that the

1. Vedānta-Sūtra II. i. 14
2. Op. cit. I. i. 4

Mīmāṁsakas rejected the worship of God. So, from this discussion also, we gather that God is an object of worship to the Mīmāṁsakas.

III. LIBERATION

Now, we proceed to ascertain the Bhāṭṭa and Prābhākara views on liberation. Let us see in the first place what Dr. Jha has said in this matter :

'There does not appear mueh difference on this important point between Kumārila and Prabhākara'.[1]

We find the Bhāṭṭa view on liberation stated in the following words :[1]

'तत्र ज्ञातात्मतत्त्वानां भोगात् पूर्वक्रियाक्षये ।
उत्तरप्रचयासत्त्वाद् देहो नोत्पद्यते पुनः ॥ 108 ॥
कर्मजन्योपभोगार्थं शरीरं न प्रवर्तते ।
तदभावे न कश्चिद्धि हेतुस्तत्रावतिष्ठते ॥ 109 ॥
मोक्षार्थी न प्रवर्तेत तत्र काम्यनिषिद्धयोः ।
नित्यनैमित्तिके कुर्यात् प्रत्यवायजिहासया ॥ 110 ॥

For those who have realised the real character of the soul, all their past karman having been exhausted by experience, and there being no further kārmic residue to wipe off, there is no further body; as the soul is burdened with a body for experiencing the result of karman, one desiring liberation should not engage in such actions as are either prohibited or enjoined with a view to material results; but, he should continue to perform those that are prescribed as necessary duties in order to avoid the sin of the neglect resulting from such duties.'[2]

---

1. Indian thought Vol. II, p. 258
2. Sambandhākṣepaparihāra, 108-10

It is necessary to notice here that this statement has been made in the Vārttika for refuting the Sāṁkhya doctrine that the knowledge of the distiction between Prakṛti and Puruṣa is the means of attaining liberation. This is stated elearly in the Nyāyaratnākara under verse 110

'Therefore a man, who desires liberation, must not stand still after having acquired the powers of discrimination, thinking that he has achieved success; but, he must proceed in such and such a manner.'

Now, we want to know what is actually intended by this verse. Does it lay down that the mere performance of compulsory and occasional duties will bring about liberation by exhausting karman, or that the knowledge of the soul is also necessary for that purpose ? We, also, want to know whether the word 'sin' in the above verse refers to the 'past karman' mentioned in verse 108 or not.

Dr. Jha is of opinion that, according to Kumārila, the knowledge of the soul is not necessary for exhausting karman. He says : 'Liberation is the absolute cessation of the body caused by the disappearance of all dharma and adharma and not by knowledge.[1]

Probably, he means to say that the knowledge of the soul plays only a subordinate part in this matter, that karman is destroyed by karman and that through the destruction of karman liberation is attained.

But, we think that in verse 110 Kumārila simply intends to propound that karman is necessary

---

1. Indian Thought Vol. II, p. 258-9

for purposes of liberation and that mere knowledge is not enough. From the following extract of the Tantravārttika, Kumārila's intention will be clear :

'आत्मज्ञानं हि संयोगपृथक्त्वात् क्रत्वर्थपुरुषार्थत्वेन ज्ञायते, तेन विना परलोकफलेषु कर्मसु प्रवृत्तिनिवृत्त्यसम्भवात् (क्रत्वर्थत्वं); तथा च य आत्मा अपहतपाप्मा विजरो विमृत्युः etc. etc., सोऽन्वेष्टव्यः स विजिज्ञासितव्यः·········तथा, आत्मानमुपासीतेति·········स्पष्टात्मज्ञानविधानापेक्षिताभ्युदयनिःश्रेयसरूपफलसम्बन्धः·········, तथा, स खल्वेवं वर्तयन् यावदायुषं ब्रह्मलोकमभिसम्पद्यते, न स पुनरावर्तते इत्यपुनरावृत्त्यात्मरूपरमात्मप्राप्त्याख्याफलवचनं (च वर्तत इति पुरुषार्थत्वम्)·········न च ज्ञानविधानेन कर्मसम्बन्धवारणम् । प्रत्याश्रमवर्णनियतानि नित्यनैमित्तिककर्माण्यपि पूर्वकृतदुरितक्षयार्थम् अकरणनिमित्तानागतप्रत्यवायपरिहारार्थञ्च कर्तव्यानि ।'[1]

'Thc knowledge of the soul is, by reason of the 'saṁyoga-pṛthaktva' maxim, known to be both kratvartha and puruṣārtha. Without that knowledge any inclination or disinclination regarding the performances which bear fruit in the next life is impossible. (Hence, it is to be regarded as kratvartha). On the other hand, there are injunctions for acquiring the knowledge of the soul which clearly require a connection with heavenly bliss or final beatitude as their fruits······'That soul which is free from sin, decrepitude, death......, he is to be sought after, he is to be known', and 'worship Ātman', as well as the text, 'He passing his whole life in this manner is sure to attain brahmaloka, he comes back no more', which states that the attainment of Paramātman is the goal from which there is no turning back. (Hence, it is to be regarded as puru-

1. Tantravārttika, pp. 240-1

ṣārtha). But, by this prescription of knowledge the connection of karman is not barred. The compulsory and the occasional duties which have been enjoined for the respective castes and orders should also be performed to destroy the sins committed in the past and to prevent the sins that will accrue from their omission'. In this extract Kumārila clearly explains his own view. So, there remains no doubt that, according to him, both jñāna and karman are necessary for attaining liberation. In the Nyāyasudhā we find a further explanation of the same view :

'ज्ञानकर्मणोः कर्मणा ज्ञानं बाध्यताम्, तुल्यत्वाद् वा विकल्पोऽस्तु, विरोधपरिहाराय वा अङ्गाङ्गिभाव परिकल्प्यतां, न तु निरपेक्ष-विहितयोः समुच्चयो युक्त इत्याशङ्क्य आह, न च ज्ञानविधानेन इति। अयमाशयः—अवान्तरकार्यैक्ये सति बाधो विकल्पो वा स्यात्, इह तु कर्मणां पूर्वकृतपापनाशः अवश्यविहिताकरणनिमित्तपापपरिहार-प्रयोजनत्वात्। निर्गुणात्मज्ञानस्य च तत्त्वप्रकाशनप्रयोजनत्वान्नावा-न्तरकार्यैक्यमपि। न च बन्धहेतुकर्मक्षयान्मोक्षसिद्धेः तत्त्व-प्रकाशनानर्थक्यं शङ्क्यं, सत्यपि पूर्वकृतकर्मक्षये कर्तृत्वभोक्तृत्वाभि-मानानिवृत्तौ निर्व्यापारत्वानुपपत्तेः अवश्यं कस्यचिद् बन्धहेतोः कर्मणः प्रसङ्गात्, तन्निवृत्त्यर्थं कर्तृत्वभोक्तृत्वाभिमाननिवृत्तेरपेक्षितताया-स्तत्त्वप्रकाशनं विनानुपपत्तेः। अतोऽवान्तरकार्यभेदान्न बाधविकल्पौ, भिन्नमार्गत्वान्नाङ्गाङ्गिभावः सम्भवतीति पारिशेष्यात् समुच्चय एव युक्तः।'[1]

'As between jñāna and karman, let the former be barred by the latter, or let there be an option owing to an equal importance of both, or to avoid a conflict let one be subservient to the other; but, as the two have been enjoined quite irrespectively of each other, it is not proper to combine them. Apprehending this (question)

1. Nyāyasudhā p. 239

he (Kumārila) says, 'by this prescription of knowledge the connection of karman is not barred'. The purport is this : if the intermediate steps be the same, an obstruction or an option may take place. But, here the intermediate steps are not the same; for, karman is required for destroying the sins committed in the past as well as for preventing the sins which may accrue owing to the non-performance of necessary duties; and, the knowledge of Nirguṇa Ātman is required for showing the true state of things. It should not be apprehended that it will be unnecessary to know the true state of things if liberation takes place on the exhaustion of karman which is the cause of bondage. The notion, 'I am the doer' or 'I am the enjoyer' lingers even after the exhaustion of the acts done in the past; and, so, it cannot be said that there is no activity. Therefore, there is every likelihood of some such karman taking place which is the cause of bondage. In order to prevent this it is necessary to put a stop to the notion, 'I am the doer' or 'I am the enjoyer'. And, that is never possible without a knowledge of the true state of things. Then, the intermediate steps being different, there is neither an obstruction nor an option. A subservience is not (also) possible, because the ways are different. Hence, the only course that remains open is combination which is accepted as reasonable' This view has been further supported by the following quotation from the Bṛhaṭ-ṭīkā :

'नित्यनैमित्तिकैरेव कुर्वाणो दुरितक्षयम् ।
ज्ञानञ्च विमलीकुर्वन्नभ्यासेन च पाचयन् ।
वैराग्यात् पक्वविज्ञानः कैवल्यं भजते नरः ॥'

'Destroying his sins by means of the performance of compulsory and occasional duties—purifying his knowledge and maturing it with repeated efforts—a man, whose knowledge grows consummate owing to absence of worldly desires, will attain liberation.'

From a consideration of all the above passages we derive the following results:—the performance of compulsory and occasional duties exhausts the acts done in the past and prevents the sins which might accrue if they were not performed; experience consumes the acts that have already begun to produce results; and the knowledge of the soul prevents the occurrence of any future 'karman' by destroying egoism, 'I am doing', etc. It is now clear that the word, **'पूर्वक्रिया'**, past 'karman', of the 108th verse does not mean the same thing as the word, **'प्रत्यवाय'**, 'sin', occurring in the 110th verse. The former means those 'karman's that have begun to produce results, while the latter means those past 'karman's which have accumulated but are still in a potential condition as well as the sins that are likely to arise from a non-performance of duties. It appears at first sight that there is likelihood of a connection between the expressions, **'ज्ञातात्मतत्त्वानाम्'** 'those that have realised the real character of the soul', and **'उत्तरप्रचयासत्त्वात्'** 'there being no further accumulation'. And, from the passages quoted from the Tantravārttika and Nyāyasudhā we learn that there is a definite connection.

So, we see that knowledge is as much necessary for destroying 'karman' as the performance of compulsory duties and thereby it serves as a necessary means for attaining salvation.

In the Bhāṭṭa-cintāmaṇi the necessity of both 'jñāna' and 'karman' is admitted; but, there is some difference as regards the details :

'अतएव ज्ञानकर्मणोः समुच्चयेन जनकता। ज्ञानेन सञ्चितानामुत्पन्नधर्माधर्माणां नाशः, नित्यकर्मभिश्च तदनुत्पत्तिः। अन्यथा नित्याकरणजन्यप्रत्यवायेन शरीरोत्पत्तिप्रसङ्गात्, तस्मादुभयोरपि शरीरोत्पत्त्यभावसम्पादकतया मोक्षजनकता।'[1]

'It is for this reason that 'jñāna' combined with 'karman' producess (liberation). The merits and demerits that have accrued already are destroyed by 'jñāna'; and, any fresh accretion of them is prevented by the performance of compulsory duties; otherwise, the sin arising from the non-performance of compulsory duties might cause the assumption of the body. As both tend to stop corporeity, both are the cause of liberation'.

Again, apprehending that knowledge alone might be regarded as sufficient to cause liberation, the author of the Bhāṭṭa-cintāmaṇi says :

'ज्ञानवतोऽपि बिहितानुष्ठाननिषिद्धाचरणाभ्यां प्रत्यवायोत्पत्तेः'।[2]

'Even a man who possesses knowledge may incur sins by neglecting necessary duties and performing prohibited acts'. From this it follows that the performance of compulsory duties stops the procreation of bodies. So, according to the Bhāṭṭa-cintāmaṇi,

1. Bhāṭṭa-cintāmaṇi p. 57.
2. Loc. cit.

knowledge destroys what is already accumulated, and 'karman' puts a stop to the future growth; but, according to the Nyāyasudhā, it is 'karman' which makes an end of what is accumulated and knowledge prevents the future growth.

In the above extract the word 'jñāna' is used in the sense of 'upāsanā' and not in the sense of the knowledge of the Nirguṇa Ātman. This becomes clear from the concluding paragraph of the same chapser which we should also quote here :

'तत्राप्युपनिषज्जन्यात्मज्ञानं दृष्टोपयोगित्वात् क्रत्वर्थम्। उपासनात्मकं तु दृष्टोपयोगाभावात्, 'सर्वान् कामानवाप्नोति, न स पुनरावर्तत' इत्यादिवाक्यशेषाच्चाभ्युदयफलकं चेति विवेकः। अतः सिद्धो ज्ञानकर्मसमुच्चयः।'

'In that case, too, the knowledge of the soul that is obtained from the Upaniṣads is 'kratvartha', because it is necessary for visible objects; but, that knowledge which is of the form of 'upāsanā' has got no visible purpose; and, there are such supplementary clauses : 'He realises all desires' and 'He does not come back'; hence, it is concluded that it (upāsanā) has heavenly bliss or liberation as its goal. So, the combination of 'jñāna' and 'karman' is established'. But, unless the word 'jñāna' in the last sentence is taken in the sense of 'upāsanā', this conclusion would by no means be appropriate.

Thus, we see that the Bhāṭṭa-cintāmaṇi differs from the Nyāyasudhā- According to the former, 'upāsanā' and 'karman' are to be combined; whereas, according to the latter, the knowledge of the Nirguṇa Ātman is to be combined with 'karman'.

In the Śāstradīpikā, also, the conclusion is that both 'jñāna' and 'karman' are necessary. We quote here the line embodying the conclusion :

'नन्वात्मज्ञानं क्रत्वर्थम् ? सत्यम् । पुरुषार्थमपि च तत्, संयोगभेदात् ।'[1]

'Is the knowledge of the soul 'kratvartha' ? Yes. And, it is 'puruṣārtha' also by an application of the saṁyoga-pṛthaktva-maxim'. But, the Śāstradīpikā, too, uses 'jñāna' in the sense of 'upāsanā', For, it is so stated in the very same place :

'यानि पुनरितिकर्तव्यताविशेषयुक्तान्युपासनात्मकानि विधीयन्ते तेषामभ्युदयनिःश्रेयसोभयफलत्वम् ।'

'Those which are enjoined with respective details as being of the nature of 'upāsanā' have both heavenly bliss and beatitude as their results'.

Here, we should notice the difference that exists between this view of the Śāstradīpikā, and the corresponding view of the Viśiṣṭādvaita system. The Viśiṣṭādvaitins hold that 'karman' is required for producing the knowledge which is preliminary to 'upāsanā', and that 'upāsanā' alone is the cause of liberation.

It is well-known that in the Advaita Bhāṣya as well as in the Viśiṣṭādvaita Bhāṣya this doctrine of the combination of 'jñāna' and 'karman' is refuted. But, there has arisen a good deal of trouble regarding the precise meaning of the word 'jñāna'. If 'jñāna' is identical with 'upāsanā', then it has been useless for the

1. Śāstradīpikā, p. 131.

Advaitins to refute the doctrine of the combination of 'jñāna' and 'karman'; for, they are never against admitting the possibility of the combination of 'upāsanā' and 'karman'. On the other hand, if the word possesses the meaning which the Advaitins attribute to it, then it has been useless on the part of the Viśiṣṭādvaitins to refute the doctrine; for, their conclusion (that 'upāsanā' alone is the cause of liberation) has nothing to do with it. So, we see that various philosophers have taken the word, 'jñāna', in various senses. Be that as it may, we have after all no doubt as to the fact that Kumārila's doctrine is one of the combination of 'jñāna' and 'karman'.

Prof. Keith has made certain observations in this connection which are not consistent with the view of the leading authorities referred to above. At one place, he says : 'But, consistently with the main view of the Mīmāṁsā, he (Kumārila) cannot admit that the Vedic texts, which seem to connect freedom from return with knowledge of the soul, mean that knowledge produces directly this result.'[1] We do not know on what foundation this statement rests; but, it clearly goes against the conclusion of the Tantravārttika and the Nyāyasudhā cited above.

In the same paragraph he makes another remark in the following words: 'It is on the contrary only possible to counteract the accumulated result of past deeds by working off the consequences'. If by 'past deeds', Prof. Keith means those deeds only which have begun to fructify, then we have nothing to say against

1. Karma-mīmāṁsā, p. 73.

his statement; but, if he means that 'karman' which has simply accumulated but has not begun to fructify, then in the light of the conclusions shown above his view cannot be regarded as correct, inasmuch as it is the performance of compulsory duties and not experience that consumes such an accumulation. Neither the Nyāyasudhā, nor the Bhāṭṭa-cintāmaṇi holds that a past accumulation is consumed by experience.

In continuation of the above extract Prof Keith further observes :

'The function of knowledge, therefore, may prevent further accumulation of merit and demerit, it cannot annul what has been accumulated. So, Kumārila attaches only an indirect value to knowledge of the self as a factor in sacrificial performance.'

This statement is self-contradictory. If, it is once admitted that knowledge prevents further accumulation of merit and demerit, how can it again be said that it has an indirect value ? We do not think that there is any difference in point of usefulness between two things of which one annuls past accumulation and the other prevents future accumulation. Both past and future accumulations are equally strong obstacles and that which serves to remove either of them must be supposed to have a direct value. We have seen above that this is the conclusion of the standard commentaries also.

It has been noticed above that Dr. Jha refers to a verse of the Ślokavārttika which shows that liberation is not to be achieved by knowledge. It runs thus :

'आत्मा ज्ञातव्य इत्येतन्मोक्षार्थं न च चोदितम्' ।[1]

'This text, 'Ātman should be known', is not enjoined with reference to liberation'. This text, however, does not stand in our way. Unfortunately, Dr. Jha has not paid any attention to the context. In this verse, Kumārila intends to propound that a knowledge of the soul is subservient to 'karman' inasmuch as it seems to induce a man to perform 'karman'. He means to say that, unless a man knows his own interests, he will not be inclined to perform 'karman'. But, this soul is the saṁsārin soul, as has been described by us in the chapter on Ātman. The Nyāyasudhā also speaks to the same effect :

'आत्मा ज्ञातव्य इत्येतन्मोक्षार्थमित्येतच्छब्दप्रयोगेन संसारिरूपात्मज्ञानस्य मोक्षार्थत्वनिरासेन कर्मप्रवृत्तिहेतुता उक्ता, असंसारिरूपात्मज्ञानस्य तु कर्मप्रवृत्त्यर्थत्वायोगात् पुरुषार्थतैव युक्ता' ।[2]

'Therefore, by the use of the word, 'एतत्' in the passage : 'आत्मा ज्ञातव्यमित्येतन्मोक्षार्थं न च चोदितम्', it is indicated that a knowledge of the saṁsārin Ātman is not necessary for liberation. And, so, it is established that it serves to create an inclination towards 'karman'. But, a knowledge of the Asaṁsārin Ātman is not necessary for creating an inclination towards 'karman' and, so, it is 'puruṣārtha'.'

There is still another passage which seems to express a contrary view :

'कर्मक्षयो हि विज्ञानादित्येतच्चाप्रमाणवत्' ।[3]

---

1. Sambandhākṣepaparihāra, 103.
2. Nyāyasudhā p. 326.
3. Op. cit. p. 96.

'There is no authority for the statement that 'karman' comes to an end through the influence of 'knowledge.' But, really there is no inconsistency. It means that 'knowledge' alone is not enough to destroy all sorts of 'karman'. In fact, it destroys the notion, 'I am the doer', etc., which is the mother of all future 'karman'.

So, the Mīmāṁsakas cannot but regard the passage of the Bhagavad-Gītā quoted in the Nyāyasudhā,

'ज्ञानाग्निः सर्वकर्माणि भस्मसात् कुरुतेऽर्जुन ।'

'O Arjuna, the fire of knowledge reduces all 'karman' to ashes', as a formal statement. In fact, it has actually been so characterised :

'कर्मनाशार्थत्वेन ज्ञानविध्यनुपलब्धेः, ज्ञानाग्निः सर्वकर्माणि भस्मसात् कुरुतेऽर्जुन इत्यादिस्मृतेरेव ओपचारिकत्वेनोपपत्तेः' :[1]

'No injunction is found which enjoins knowledge for destroying 'karman', and the Smṛti texts such as :

'O Arjuna, the fire of knowledge reduces all 'karman' to ashes', etc., can be explained as figurative expressions'.

According to the Sāṁkhya doctrine, knowledge in the shape of discrimination between Prakṛti and Puruṣa is the cause of liberation; according to the Advaita doctrine, mere knowledge of Ātman is the cause of liberation; and according to the Bhāṭṭa doctrine, a combination of knowledge and 'karman' is the cause of liberation.

There is, thus, a difference between the Bhāṭṭa view and the Advaita view in this respect Though we have

1. Nyāyasudhā p. 329.

shown before that there is no difference between the views of the two systems regarding the form of Ātman or the existence of Nirguṇa Brahman, yet this difference does not create any conflict, as the matters are quite different. There may have been an agreement as to the conceptions of Ātman or God; but, that is no reason why there should be agreement as regards the means of liberation. Or, it may be supposed that there is an agreement of opinion. It may be that Kumārila really prefers knowledge, but outwardly propounds that 'karman' and 'jñāna' are of equal importance, only to show respect for 'karman'. If, this view is accepted as correct, there will remain no difference at all between the two doctrines. We shall presently try to show that Kumārila's conception of liberation is not different from the Advaita conception.

The Prābhākara view of the process of attaining liberation is the same as the Bhāṭṭa view. Dr. Jha has given a description of the process in accordance with the view of the Prābhākaras. It tallies exactly with the doctrine of the combination of 'jñāna' and 'karman'. It is given in the following lines of Dr. Jha, which are a literal translation of the following paragraph of the Prakaraṇa-pañcikā :

'यः खलु सांसारिकेभ्यो दुःखेभ्य ;उद्विग्नस्तदनुषङ्गशवलेभ्यश्च सुखेभ्योऽपि गतस्पृहो मोक्षायोत्तिष्ठते, स तावद् बन्धहेतुभूतेभ्यो निषिद्धेभ्यः प्रत्यवायहेतुभूतेभ्योऽभ्युदयसाधनेभ्यश्च निवर्तमानः सन्, उत्पन्नपूर्वौ धर्माधर्मौ कृतावपि भोगेन क्षयं नयन्, शमदमब्रह्मचर्याद्योपबृंहितेनात्मज्ञानेन, न च पुनरावर्तत इत्यपुनरावृत्तये चोदितेन, निःशेषकर्माशयं नाशयन् मुच्यते; न चापुनरावृत्तेरर्थवादतया वर्णनमात्मज्ञानस्यापरार्थत्वात् ।'[1]

1. Prakaraṇa-pañcikā, p. 157

'As to how all this comes about, the following explanation is given : (1) First, the man becomes disgusted with the troubles that he has to undergo during mundane existence; (2) secondly, finding the pleasures of the world also to be invariably accompanied by some sort of pain, he comes to lose all interest in and longing for pleasures also; (3) thirdly, he turns his attention towards liberation; (4) fourthly, he ceases to perform such deeds as are prohibited and which lead to trouble, as also from those that are prescribed only as leading to some sort of happiness here or hereafter; (5) fifthly, he attenuates all previously accrued 'dharma' and 'adharma' by undergoing the experiences resulting from them; and (6) sixthly, he destroys the sole receptacle or abode of his experiences by the knowledge of the soul along with such auxiliaries as contentment, self-control, and so forth. All these are laid down in the Scriptures as tending to put a stop to the further return of that soul to the world; and, it is only when all this has happened that the soul is free. The Vedic texts, speaking of the non-return to this world, cannot he regarded as mere 'arthavāda'; because, the knowledge of the soul not being laid down as subservient to anything else, the result spoken of must be regarded as a qualification for the man entitled to that knowledge.'[1]

So, we agree fully with Dr. Jha in the opinion that there does not appear to be much difference on this important point between Kumārila and Prabhākara; but, we cannot pursuade ourselves to accept the state-

1. Indian Thought Vol. II, pp. 257-58

ment—'and 'not by knowledge' adds Kumārila, etc.,' as correct.

WHAT IS LIBERATION ?

We have hitherto tried to ascertain the process of attaining liberation as promulgated by the Mīmāṁsakas, and we shall now proceed to determine what they understand by the term 'liberation'.

There are some who think that, according to Kumārila, liberation consists in the enjoyment of constant bliss. They believe that 'manas' exists in liberation. This view has been cited in the Śāstradīpikā.[1] But, the author of the Śāstradīpikā as well as some others are of opinion that liberation is of a negative character. They hold that there cannot be an enjoyment of bliss as 'manas' does not exist at that time, and that it is nothing but a mere cessation of pain. But, to us the view that liberation means the existence of Ātman by itself as characterised by the cessation of all pain, appears to be the true view of Kumārila; for, this view is propounded in the Tantravārttika and the Nyāyasudhā. In the Tantravārttika we find :

'न स पुनरावर्तत इत्यपुनरावृत्त्यात्मकपरमात्मप्राप्त्यवस्था-फलवचनम्'[2]

'The text—'He does not come back'—indicates the result in the shape of the attainment of Paramātman which is nothing but non-return.' This expression,

1. Śāstradīpikā, pp. 126–7
2. Tantravārttika, p. 241

'attainment of Paramātman' of Kumārila, has thus been explained in the Nyāyasudhā :

'शरीरसम्बन्धोपाधिककर्तृत्वभोक्तृत्वात्मकसंसारिरूपावस्थापरि - त्यागेन अकर्तृभोक्तृत्वात्मकासंसारिरूपनिजावस्थाया एव परमात्मप्राप्तिरूपत्वेन तस्या अवस्थाया अजन्यत्वाद् युक्तमक्षयत्वम्'

The attainment of Paramātman means nothing but the existence of Asaṁsārin Ātman, as it is without any such notion as 'I am doing', 'I am enjoying', etc., which is brought about by shaking off the saṁsārin form which is possessed with the sense, 'I am doing', 'I am enjoying', etc., and which is characterised by its connection with a body. As that condition is not artificial, it is to be regarded as eternal'. From this it follows that liberation is the same thing as the pure existence of Ātman marked by freedom from pain. This freedom from pain can be brought about by the annihilation of 'karman' and not by a power of discrimination as is propounded by the Sāṁkhyas.

This view is not inconsistent with the purport of another statement of Kumārila :

'न ह्यभावात्मकं मुक्त्वा मोक्षनित्यत्वकारणम्'[1]

'Liberation cannot be regarded as eternal unless it is of a negative character,'—for (in this view) it is not admitted that the pure state of Ātman is possible without cessation of pain. The above verse is meant of refute the view of the Sāṁkhyas, in which happiness is supposed to spring directly from the power of discrimination; but, it is not directed against those who hold that liberation which is a pure state of Ātman

1. Sambandhākṣepaparihāra, 107

is due to the annihilation of 'karman' and cessation of pain. The latter do not assert that liberation is a state of Ātman consisting in the enjoyment of happiness, which is a thing that is caused. Herein lies the significance of the qualifying clause, 'अपुनरावृत्त्यात्मक-' 'consisting in non-return,' used in the Tantravārttika. It indicates that the non-return which is established by the Upaniṣad text, 'He does not come back,' is the same thing as the attainment of Brahman. The Nyāyasudhā expresses this clearly in the following words :

'अपुनरावृत्तेर्ब्रह्मप्राप्तितो भेदनिरासाय अपुनरावृत्त्यात्मकता उक्ता'[1]

'It is said to consist in non-return only in order to do away with the distinction between non-return and the attainment of Brahman.'

Kumārila regards liberation not as mere cessation of pain but as the Asaṁsārin state of Ātman in which there is no such sense as 'I am enjoying', 'I am doing', etc. According to the view in which liberation is cessation of pain., Ātman does not lose such notions as 'I am doing,' 'I am enjoying,' etc., and is not Nirguṇa (as in the view of the Naiyāyikas), whereas according to the other view, Ātman loses such notions and is Nirguṇa at that time. The following extract from Prof. Keith's work shows that he accepts this latter view as the original view of the Mīmāṁsā : 'The final condition, then, of man will be the persistence

---

1. Nyāyasudhā p. 323

of pure consciousness but without cognition or feeling of any sort.'[1]

If, it is supposed that the author of the Śāstradīpikā means that liberation is the state of Nirguṇa Ātman characterised by cessation of pain, then, there will remain no difference between the two views, though he says that it is cessation of pain.

The Advaitins also regard liberation as the state of Nirguṇa Ātman marked by cessation of pain. So, there is no difference in this respect between the Advaitins and Kumārila. The Bhāṭṭas, unlike the Prābhākaras, do not deny the authoritativeness of those Vedic texts which speak of existing (सिद्ध) things; and, hence, the Bhāṭṭas feel no difficulty in recognising the pure state of Nirguṇa Ātman which is otherwise known as the state of the Highest Bliss. The Prābhākaras regard only those texts as authoritative which lay down duties. So, it is not possible for them to conform to the view that Ātman in the state of the Highest Bliss is free. In the Prakaraṇa-pañcikā, we find that this view has been refuted on the ground that it is not the function of the Vedic texts to state perfect (सिद्ध) things. We quote here the exact words :

'परमानन्दताभ्युपगमोऽपि मन्दफल एव, न च प्रमाणमपि तत्रैव अवकल्पते, श्रुतीनां सिद्धवस्तुबोधकत्वाभावात्'[2]

'It is no good admitting the attainment of the state of the Highest Bliss, nor is there any authority on this point; as the Vedic texts do not stand for describing

1. Karma-mīmāṁsā, pp. 73-4
2. Prakaraṇa-pañcikā, p. 153

perfect things.' From this we understand that, in the Bhāṭṭa view, it is possible to regard liberation as the state of the Highest Bliss. According to the Prābhākaras, the mere cessation of pain is liberation. So, there is a distinction between the two views. Dr. Jha has said that both are agreed as to their view of liberation[1]. But, on a consideration of all the views cited and discussed above, it is not possible for us to accept this observation of Dr. Jha as valid.

It is necessary to point out here that the state of the Highest Bliss and enjoyment of happiness are not the same thing. The following passage of Kumārila shows that enjoyment of happiness is not a permanent thing :

'सुखोपभोगरूपश्च यदि मोक्षः प्रपद्यते।
स्वर्ग एव भवेदेष पर्यायेण, क्षयी च सः ॥'[2]

'If it is admitted that liberation consists in the enjoyment of happiness, it will merely become another name for paradise,—such a thing is transient.' But, the state of the Highest Bliss is a permanent thing. So, the above statement of Kumārila does not stand in the way of recognising such a state as liberation. This has also been indicated in the passages of the Nyāyasudhā quoted above.

Dr. Jha has observed that there is an agreement between the two schools regarding the conception of liberation and that there is a difference as regards the process of attaining it. We, on the contrary, find that there is a difference of opinion regarding the conception and that there is an agreement regarding the process.

1. Indian Thought, Val. II. p. 259
2. Sambandhākṣapaparihāra, 105

APPLICATION OF MĪMĀṀSĀ MAXIMS TO HINDU LAW

APPLICATION OF MĪMĀṀSĀ MAXIMS TO HINDU LAW

The importance of the Mīmāṁsā rules as regards the interpretation of the Hindu Law is very high. We cannot make a better estimate of it than what Sir John Edge[1] has done with reference to a question of Hindu Law arising before him. 'The question is,' says he, 'how are the texts of Vaśiṣṭha to be construed. It must clearly be construed according to the rules for the construction of the texts of the sacred books of the Hindu Law, if authoritative rules on the subject exist. That rules for the construction of the sacred texts and law of the Hindus do exist cannot be disputed, although those rules have been frequently overlooked or not referred to by Judges or English text-writers, probably because they are in Sanskrit, and have, so for as I am aware, not yet been translated. That they are rules of the highest authority is obvious from the manner in which they have been referred to by Mr. Colebrooke.'[2]

It is a matter of regard that though Mr. Colebrooke pointed out the importance of the Mīmāṁsā rules of interpretation long, long ago, still proper attention was not paid to them by the Courts of Justice in subsequent times. A proper application of these rules might have produced different results in many a Hindu Law

---

1. Chief Justice, Allahabad High Court.
2. Indian Law Reports 14 Allahabad p. 70

case. Rules of interpretation possess an importance in respect of the Hindu Law, much greater than in respect of the law of any other country. The Hindu Law has never been regarded as man-made law. It is contained in the sacred books. The administration of it has always been more or less in the absolute charge of learned men who were to derive the law from the texts only. So, interpretations were necessary at every step, which could never be carried on consistently without fixed rules of interpretation. It may be said that the Mīmāṁsā rules were framed for the purpose of construing Vedic passages only; and, so, they are not applicable to the civil law. To this two answers may be given. In the first place, the law contained in the texts of the Smṛtis is presumned to follow entirely from the Vedas. According to the orthodox traditions, all texts of the Smṛtis had corresponding texts in the Vedas, many of which are now lost.[1] The distinction between the sacred law and the secular law is not recognised by the orthodox Hindu mind. The Smṛtis are regarded as an off-shoot of the Vedas. Hence, the Mīmāṁsā rules which are applied to the Vedic texts are also equally applicable to the Smṛti texts. Secondly, a rule is always a rule. It will, as a matter of course, govern a case which comes within its purview, no matter whether it is a question of sacred or secular law. The logic of the Mīmāṁsā is the logic of law and is capable of a very wide application. In fact, all commentators and digest-makers of the Smṛtis have copiously cited the maxims of the Mīmāṁsā in their works for settling controversial points.

1. Adhikaraṇa I. iii. 1

We find the following statement in the commentary of Śabara on the authoritativeness of Smṛti texts. Hence, those (injunctions) which have apparent objects in view are authoritative on that ground and those which have no apparent objects are to be supposed to have been based on Vedic texts.[1] Now, by this statement, it is not meant that all such Smṛti texts as enjoin the following of one's preceptor, etc., are not based on the Vedas, merely because their objects are apparent; but, even such texts are to be supposed to have had a Vedic origin without which no 'niyama' would be possible. The Tantravārttika, also, says to the same effect :

'यत्तु भाष्यकारेण दृष्टार्थत्वात् प्रामाण्यमित्युक्तं, तत् पूर्वपक्षवादितिशयार्थम्। एतदुक्तं भवति यास्तावद् अदृष्टार्थाः स्मृतयस्ताः काश्चिद्-प्रमाणीकुर्याद् भवान्, इमाः पुनर्गुर्वनुगमनादिविषयाः कथमिवाप्रमाणं भविष्यन्ति ।[2]

'In stating that certain things are authoritative because they have apparent objects, the commentator intends to silence his opponents. The position may be explained thus : you may not recognise the authority of those texts which do not indicate any apparent object; but, how can you ignore the value of those texts which prescribe the following of one's preceptor, etc., (which indicate apparent objects) ?'

A duty which produces a worldly benefit attracts people naturally and one may not like to know whether it has any other sanction or not. But, if we consider

---

1. Adhikaraṇa, 1. iii. 1
2. Tantravārttika, p. 78

the matter from another point of view, the existence of a further sanction will be manifest. What would be the consequence if you omit to perform such a duty ? Would an omission end in a mere loss of the expected benefit, or produce a sin also ? The following extract from the Nyāyasudhā makes the point clear.

'निष्पन्नविद्यैरप्यनुष्ठीयमानस्य गुर्वनुगमनादेर्दृष्टार्थत्वायोगादवश्यकर्तव्यतान्यथानुपपत्तेरकरणनिमित्तप्रत्यवायपरिहार्यत्वावसायात् तस्य चानन्यप्रमाणत्वाद् वेदमूलत्वसिद्धिः ।'[1]

'To such acts, as the following of one's preceptor, etc., which are performed even by people who have finished their educational career, no earthly motive can be ascribed. But, the compulsory character of such duties cannot be otherwise established than by holding that it is necessary to avoid the sin that would accrue from non-performance; and, as there is no other authority to warrant this conclusion, it is admitted that the texts prescribing such duties have had a Vedic origin.'

It is enjoined in the Smṛtis that a pupil must follow the preceptor and so forth. So long as the preceptor teaches the pupil, the latter is certainly interested in pleasing the former by following him, etc. But, when the course of study is finished and the pupil does not want any further favour from his preceptor, there is no necessity for pleasing the latter. But, in fact, it is found that people who have finished their educational course behave themselves in the same manner towards their ex-preceptors as they did when they were students.

---

1. Nyāyasudhā, p. 126

They would never do so unless such duties were compulsory. But, this idea of compulsion can emanate only from the Vedas and from no other authority; and, hence, such injunctions of the Smṛtis are supposed to have a Vedic origin.

Now, we see that the duty of following one's preceptor is not only compulsory for a pupil who has to win favours from his preceptor but it is also compulsory for one who expects no such gain. If the duty be not carried out, a sin would accrue to both alike. Hence, it is concluded that a Vedic sanction is to be suppossed for all injunctions of the Smṛtis having or not having apparent intention. Those injunctions, which deal with tangible, worldly objects, are ordinarily regarded as 'secular law', while those injunctions which deal with no such objects are regarded as 'religious law'. But, both of them, as we have seen above, are to be regarded as off-shoots of the Vedic law.

The sage, Yājñavalkya, has made it binding upon kings to try cases in accordance with the rules of the Dharmaśāstra, as will appear from the following passage :

व्यवहारान् नृपः पश्येद् विद्वद्भिर्ब्राह्मणैः सह ।
धर्मशास्त्रानुसारेण क्रोधलोभविवर्जितः ॥[1]

'The king shall try cases, together with learned Brāhmins, according to the Dharmaśāstra and without giving vent to anger or greed.' Yājñavalkya himself has drawn a distinction between Dharmaśāstra and Arthaśāstra. It is clear from the manner in which he

1. Vyavahāra, V. 1

has used the expression 'Arthaśāstra', as also from the interpretations of the Mitākṣarā, that it means those rules of law which entail visible worldly results. Vijñāneśvara has interpreted it as धर्मशास्त्रान्तर्गतमेव अर्थशास्त्रम् i.e., it is nothing foreign to the Dharmaśāstra but a part of it. Still, apprehending that some cases might be tried as cases of secular law according to the principles of common sense, etc., Yajñavalkya enjoins that all cases are to be tried according to the law of the Dharmaśāstra. But, the law of the Dharmaśāstra is an off-shoot of the Vedic law which is interpreted and adjusted according to the rules and principles of the Mīmāṁsā. These rules and principles, therefore, are to be adopted for interpreting and adjusting the law of the Dharmaśāstra also. Now, the law of the Dharmaśāstra includes rules of pure religious Law as well as rules dealing with worldly matters. Hence, the rules and principles of the Mīmāṁsā are to be applied to both of them. The Mīmāṁsā maxims are particularly to be applied to cases in which there arises a conflict between different Smṛti texts. The following line of Yājñavalkya Smṛti shows the importance that is attached to the Mīmāṁsā maxims.

'स्मृत्योर्विरोधे न्यायस्तु बलवान् व्यवहारतः'[1]

'When Smṛti texts conflict wilh one another, the principles or decisions of the Mīmāṁsā, which have been adopted in practice, will prevail.' The word, 'nyāya' seems to mean ordinary rules of practice or equitable principles; but, on a proper consideration we cannot accept this meaning as adequate. It is not fair

1. Vyavahāra, V. 21

to suggest that ordinary rules of practice or equitable principles should be regarded as the decisive factors in settling disputed points of religious law. Had 'nyāya' meant ordinary rules of practice or equitable principles, it would not have been necessary to use both, 'nyāya' and vyavahāra,' having the same meaning, in the same sentence. But, our interpretation of the word is free from such a difficulty. The maxims of the Mīmāṁsā are not strange things; but, they have been arrived at by applying the general principles of logic to various knotty cases of Vedic law. It is for this reason that in the Mitākṣarā the word 'nyāya' has been interpreted as being of the form of general rules and exceptions. Just as the rulings laid down by the higher courts of law are accepted as authorities for settling points of modern law, so the 'nyāyas' of the Mīmāṁsā which have been actually adopted in practice are invoked for settling points of Smṛti law. That 'nyāya' means a Mīmāṁsā maxim or decision is borne out by the following passage of the Bhāṭṭadīpikā—'सन्न्यायविरोधे स्मृतिरप्रमाणम्'. If a Smṛti text is in conflict with a 'sannyāya' it loses its binding force.' The expression 'sannyāya' has been explained in the Prabhāvalī[1] as nothing other than a Mīmāṁsā-nyāya.

In the Śāstradīpikā, also, it has been held that such texts of the Kalpa-Sūtras, as जाघनीभिः पत्नीः संयाजयन्ति etc., have no binding authority, inasmuch as they go against the decisions of the Mīmāṁsā. Besides, it is not at all probable that such high importance should have been attached to popular maxims or principles.

1. Prabhāvali, 1. iii. 5

Hence, we conclude that in the above passage of Yājñavalkya, स्मृत्योर्विरोधे न्यायस्तु, the word 'nyāya' does not mean a popular or equitable principle but a maxim or decision of the Mīmāṁsā.

Thus, we see that we have to depend upon the maxims and decisions of the Mīmāṁsā for the interpretation of Smṛti law and for reconciling its conflicting views. We shall, next, proceed to show how the Mīmāṁsā 'nyāya's are actually applied to concrete cases. 'Adoption', says Prof. Keith, 'affords a fruitful field for the application of Mīmāṁsā principles.' We propose, therefore, to interpret certain Smṛti texts relating to adoption in the light of the Mīmāṁsā principles. The text of the Smṛti, which speaks of adoption, runs thus :

'अपुत्रेणैव कर्तव्यः पुत्रप्रतिनिधिः सदा'

'A sonless person must always take a substitute for a son.'

The expression 'aputreṇa', here, is in the masculine gender. The question strikes one at once as to whether a male person only is entitled to adopt, or the expression includes a female also. Exactly the same question arose in the case of the Vedic injunction, स्वर्गकामो यजेत, 'one who desires to enjoy heaven, shall perform a sacrifice.' There, too, the expression, स्वर्ग-कामः, is in the masculine gender. The Adhikaraṇa in which the matter has been discussed is thus summarised in the Śāstradīpikā :

'तत्र पुंलिङ्गनिर्देशात् पुंस एवाधिकारिता ।
प्रकृत्यर्थतया लिङ्गं संख्यावन्नाविवक्षितम् ॥'[1]

'As the word denoting the agent is characterised by the masculine gender, a male person only is entitled (to perform a sacrifice); the gender is included in the meaning of the base; and, so, it cannot be said that the gender is not intended as the number.' This is the pūrva-pakṣa or the prima facie view of the case. On this the conclusion is :

'प्रकृत्यर्थोऽपि खल्वेतदुद्देश्यस्य विशेषणम् ।
संख्यया तुल्यनीतित्वान् न विवक्षां प्रपद्यते ॥'

'Though this (gender) is included in the meaning of the base, still it qualifies the subject (and not the predicate); its position is in no way different from that of the number; and, hence, it is not intended.' Thus, this Adhikaraṇa removes the ineligibility of a wife so far as the performance of a sacrifice is concerned and there can be no objection to applying the same principle to the case of adoption, too.

Now, another question arises here as to whether this eligibility would be joint or separate. On this point a discussion has been made in the next Adhikaraṇa[2] and the decision is that the wife alone is not entitled to perform a sacrifice. So, in the case of adoption, too, the wife alone would not be entitled to adopt. In the Adhikaraṇa referred to above, it has been first argued that the husband and the wife are separately entitled to perform a sacrifice, as the expression 'svarga-

1. Śāstradīpikā VI. i. 2
2. VI. i. 4

kāmaḥ' (one who desires to enjoy heavenly bliss), is in the singular number. But, this argument is not satisfactory. To complete a sacrifice the husband and the wife have to perform certain specific duties as आज्यावेक्षण, etc.; and, so, they have to depend upon each other. If they proceed separately the performance of each will be defective. Hence, the conclusion is that the right to perform a sacrifice is a joint right. From this it follows that a wife by herself has no right to perform any duty in which the co-operation of the husband is necessary. But, the digest-makers have decided that a wife who has obtained permission from her husband is entitled to adopt. The authority for this decision is the following text of Vaśiṣṭha :

'न स्त्री पुत्रं दद्यात् प्रतिगृह्णीयाद्वा, अन्यत्र अनुज्ञानाद् भर्तुः ।'

'The wife must not give or take a son in adoption without the permission of her husband.' This text clearly implies that with the permission of the husband the wife is competent to adopt. So, a special provision is made by this particular Smṛti-text and not on any general principle.

It may be asked here if the performance of a sacrifice and the adoption of a son are exactly similar cases in so far as the co-operation or the mutual help of the husband and the wife is necessary. To this the answer would be that co-operation is as much necessary in the one case as in the other. The following passage throws some light on this matter.

'अग्न्याधानादिकं तत्र कृत्वाज्योत्पवनान्तकम् ।
दातुः समक्षं गत्वा तु पुत्रं देहीति याचयेत् ॥'

'After performing all the rites from 'agnyādhāna' up to 'ājyotpavana', (he) shall approach the giver and beg with the words 'Give your son'.

The rite, agnyādhāna, that is mentioned in this passage is possible only in the case of a husband who possesses the sacred fire as well as the wife, and not in the case of wife.

In the Śāstradipikā we find a decision which is embodied in the following words :

'प्रोषिते अन्यकर्मव्यापृते वा यजमाने ये तावदाज्यावेक्षणादय-स्तेष्वध्वर्य्वादयः कर्तारः ।'[1]

'If the sacrificer has gone to a distant place or is engaged in any other sacrifice, the 'adhvaryu' and others (perists) will be entitled to perform the (his) rites of 'ājyāvekṣaṇa', etc.' On the strength of this statement it may be maintained that a wife whose husband has gone to a distant land is entitled to adopt, as her husband is alive and as his fire is present. But, when the husband is dead, how can his widow who does not possess, nor has the capacity to possess the sacred fire, be allowed to perform a ceremony in which the use of the sacred fire is compulsory. After the death of the husband the widow cannot keep the sacred fire for her own sake. On the other hand, a man whose wife is dead, may, if he so likes, preserve the sacred fire for his own sake, which will be regarded as a representative of his deceased wife. Hence, it may rather be possible for such a widower to adopt.

1. VI. iii. 7

Thus, we see that according to the decisions of the Mīmāṁsā a wife is only allowed to exercise her right to adopt a son jointly with her husband. In the text of Manu **'माता पिता वा दद्यातां यमद्भिः पुत्रमापदि'**[1] 'the son whom the father and the mother give in distress,' the word, **वा**, has been taken to mean 'and'; for, otherwise, the use of the verb in the dual number, **'दद्याताम्'** would not be appropriate; and, so, this text points to the joint right of the husband and the wife. The text, **'दद्यान् माता पिता वा यं स पुत्रो दत्तको भवेत्'**[2] 'the son whom the father or the mother gives will become the adopted son,' seems to establish a separate right for the father as well as for the mother. But, in fact, it is not so. The words, father and mother, do not mean here any father or any mother; but, they are to be taken in a qualified sense. The word, father, means, as we have shown above, a father whose wife is dead but who still preserves the sacred fire; and, the word, mother, means a mother whose husband has gone to a distant place. We do not obtain anything else from the decisions of the Mīmāṁsā. In the Mitākṣarā the word, mother, has been taken to include a widowed mother also. The view of the Mitākṣarā is not based on any decision of the Mīmāṁsā but is obtained by combining this text of Yājñavalkya with the text **'अन्यत्रानुज्ञानाद् भर्तुः'** ।

At any rate the commentators have not regarded this text of Yājñavalkya as establishing the existence of a separate right of the mother. The interpretation

1. Manu IX. 168
2. Yājñavalkya, Vyavahāra, 130

of the Mitākṣarā shows that the mother cannot exercise her right independently. In it the word, 'mother' has been interpreted as a mother whose husband is either dead or gone to a distant place and who is permitted by her husband. If the mother possessed an independent right it would not be necessary to put all these qualifications. The Mitākṣarā does not even say that the mother can give in the presence of the father with his permission. The observation of Mr. Gopal Chandra Sarker - 'In any view of the Law, the wife is competent to give her son in adoption, when her husband is alive, and is capable of giving his consent, only with his assent'[1] will be consistent with the Mitākṣarā, only if by the word 'alive' he means 'प्रोषितः;' otherwise, there will be an inconsistency. The Mitākṣarā adds a third alternative, 'उभाभ्यां वा' or by both the parents.' We have said adove that this view only is in accordance with the Mīmāṁsā doctrine of the joint eligibility of a married couple, while a separate exercise of the right by the mother after her husband's death follows from some Smṛti texts only.

As regard the right of the mother Mr. Golap Chandra Sarker further says : 'According to the ancient law, however, the father had in addition to the natural right the patria potestas, and the mother's status was similar to that of a minor wanting discretion; hence, the father could exercise the right of gift, independently of the mother, who could not exercise such a right unless her want of discretion were supplied by the assent of her husband : this appears to be the

1. Hindu Law of Adoption p. 276

substance of Vaśiṣṭha's text.'[1] These remarks of Mr. Sarker are quite in harmony with the ancient rules of practice. If a wife is disobedient her husband is entitled to perform a sacrifice without her co-operation; but, when the husband is unwilling the wife cannot ignore him and proceed to perform a sacrifice without his help. A woman is not allowed to enjoy so much freedom. The text, **न स्त्री स्वातन्त्र्यमर्हति**, 'a woman is not worthy of freedom,' stands in her way. But, although a man, whose wife shows disobedience, is allowed to perform a sacrifice independently of his wife, still neither a bachelor nor a widower, who does not preserve a sacred fire, is ever allowed to perform a sacrifice. There is no reason why the same rules should not apply to the case of adoption.

In the texts of Manu and Yājñavalkya we find the words, **दद्याताम्** and **दद्यात्**, both of which are derived from the root, **दा**, which means to give. Hence, it follows that the status of the boy as an adopted son is due to **दान**. Now, it may be asked here whether this status of the boy would arise at all, if he is made over by a person who in not permitted by the Śāstras to do so. To answer this question it becomes necessary for us to ascertain in the first place whether the sonship of an adopted son is merely a social status or it is the result of a religious sacrament. Vijñāneśvara is silent on this point; but, in the Vyavahāra-mayūkha it has been held that the sonship of an adopted son is 'adṛṣṭa'; because, such a son is not produced by the combination of seed and blood. Neither any commentator nor any digest-maker has ever challenged this conclusion. Hence, we may take it for granted that it is approved by all, by reason of the maxim that what is not prohibited is accepted. When it is said that the status of an adopted son, which is an adṛṣṭa caused by a gift, it is implied as a matter of course that the gift includes all ceremonies up to the acceptance. The mere act of acceptance cannot create this adṛṣṭa or invisible sonship. So, the 'dattaka-homa' and other religious rites are required to be performed. These rites are regarded as parts of the act of acceptance.

Again, if the sonship of an adopted son is regarded as adṛṣṭa it will be possible only in the case of such a boy as is recommended in the Śāstras for this purpose. He, with regard to whom gift and acceptance are prescribed, is the only person fit for the consecration. In the injunction 'मुद्गान् प्रोक्षति' 'sprinkles water upon the 'mudga'-beans, the act of sprinkling water is regarded as an act of consecration, and 'mudga'-beans are the object fit for it. If 'mudga' be not available, can 'māṣa', which is a similar species of corn, be used instead of it? There is a rule in the Mīmāṁsā that, if an article is not available, a similar article may be used in its stead.[1] So, 'māṣa' which can serve all the practical purposes of 'mudga'-beans might be used instead of it. But, it has been held in the sixth chapter[2] of the Mīmāṁsā that 'māṣa' cannot be so used; because, the use of 'māṣa' in a sacrifice is prohibited by a special text, अयज्ञिया वै माषाः, चणकाः कोद्रवाः', 'Māṣa, caṇaka and kodrava' are not fit to be used in a sacrifice.' It was argued that 'māṣa' would be used here not as 'māṣa' but

1. Mīmāṁsādhikaraṇa VI. iii. 4
2. Op. cit. VI. iii. 6

as a substitute for 'mudga'; and, so,'māṣa'may be allowed. But, that argument has been refuted by the counter-argument that, whether 'māṣa' comes as 'māṣa' or as a substitute for 'mudga', it comes to be used in a sacrifice; and, when its use in a sacrifice is prohibited, it cannot be used on any account. So, though 'māṣa' can meet all the apparent purposes of 'mudga', still it cannot be used in a sacrifice, and why ? Because, there is an invisible element involved therein. When 'māṣa' is declared to be unfit, it is understood that the invisible merit arising from the sprinkling of water will not be produced in 'māṣa'; and, hence, the sacrifice will be defective; otherwise, there could be no earthly objection to the use of 'māṣa' in the absence of 'mudga'.

Similarly, a child, such as an only son, whose gift and acceptance are prohibited in the Smṛti texts, is not fit for adoption. Such a child may be competent for all practical purposes; but, when he is declared unfit by the Śāstras we must understand that his gift and acceptance will not create the necessary invisible element in the status of an adopted son. By making the gift, the father may lose his dominion over the child and the recipient may acquire a dominion over him (i.e., he may be regarded as a chattel or a slave of the person who adopts the child); but, he will not become the son of him who adopts him. He will neither be entitled to offer piṇḍas nor to inherit the properties of the person who adopts him. In the Dattaka-Mīmāṁsā it is decided that an adopted son of whom all the sacramental ceremonies up to the ceremony of tonsure have been performed in the natural father's family will become a slave of the adopter and not a son. From this it follows that mere gift and acceptance cannot confer the status of sonship on an adoptee in whose case gift and acceptance are prohibited. Medhātithi says that the sonship of an adopted son, etc. is due to an unseen merit. And, just as wifehood is created by the performance of particular religious rites, so is the sonship of an adopted son.

It might be suggested here that, by the violation of a prohibition, a sin only would be committed, but the due result would not be annulled; for, in the Adhikaraṇa relating to the performance of a prohibited act[1] it has been decided that such a performance would only produce a sin. In that Adhikaraṇa the injunction that is discussed is 'न कलञ्जं भक्षयेत्' 'do not eat kalañja'. It would be absurd to suppose that if anybody violates this prohibition and eats 'kalañja' he will not feel the natural results of eating the thing, viz., satisfaction, nutrition, etc. Hence, it is concluded that in this case a violation would cause sin only. By applying this principle it might be argued that in spite of a prohibition, gift and acceptance would cause sonship. But, this argument would be very cogent if the sonship of an adopted son were a perceptible fact like satisfaction due to eating. But, we have shown above that it is not so. A tangible result may be produced by any man at any time by adopting a proper process of performance, but, as regards an invisible result we cannot know from our experience how it is to be produced. Hence, we can by no means assert that an act perform-

1. Adhikaraṇa VI ii. 5

ed by a person who is not permitted by the Śāstras or at a time which is not recommended, will produce an invisible result. In the Bhāmatī we find :

'न हि अनधिकारिणा समर्थेनापि कृतं कर्म फलाय कल्पते वैश्यस्तोम इव राजन्यब्राह्मणाभ्याम् ।'

'An act done by a person, who, though able, yet unauthorised, is not supposed to produce the result like the Vaiśyastoma performed by a Kṣatriya or a Brāhmin. A Brāhmin or a Kṣatriya can perform the sacrifice which a Vaiśya is entitled to perform; but, the former is not authorised to perform it. So, if a Brāhmin or a Kṣatriya performs it, the proper result will not be achieved. The same decision is made in the Pūrva-Mīmāṁsā regarding the performance of a sacrifice by a Śūdra. In the Apa-śūdrādhikaraṇa[1] it has been held that a Śūdra is not authorised to perform a sacrifice. If an act done by an unauthorised person could produce the proper result, there would be no reason why a Śūdra should not be able to achieve the desired result by performing a sacrifice; and, then, there would not be any necessity for introducing this Adhikaraṇa at all. So, we see that there is a clear difference between the eating of 'kalañja' and the gift and acceptance in adoption.

In the Viśvajit sacrifice, the sacrificer is required to give away all that he possesses. But, it has been decided in the Mīmāṁsā[2] that one's father and similar other relations cannot be given. On this point the Śāstra-dīpikā observes :

---

1. VI. i. 7
2. VI. vii. 1

'स्वत्वत्यागपूर्वकं हि परस्वत्वापादनं दानं, न च दीयमानोऽपि पिता न पिता भवति ।'[1]

'A gift is the creation of the right of another person after relinquishing one's own right; a father will not become no-father even if he is given away.' From this it follows that a mere gift neither extinguishes nor creates fatherhood, sonship, husbandhood, etc. One may give or sell a box or a table to another person; and, by the transaction the right of ownership that belonged to the former may be transferred to the latter. But, it is not possible to give or sell a wife so as to make her the wife of another person. If a mere gift or an acceptance could create sonship, there would be no necessity for the performance of 'homa', etc.

The following text of Vaśiṣṭha implies that the sonship of an adopted son is different even from ordinary sonship :

'शुक्रशोणितसम्भवः पुरुषो मातापितृनिमित्तकः, तस्य प्रदान-विक्रयपरित्यागेषु मातापितरौ प्रभवतः ।'

'A person is the product of virile seed and uterine blood, caused by the father and the mother; the father and the mother are competent to give, sell or abandon him'. From the epithet, 'शुक्रशोणितसम्भवः', we understand that it is only the natural parents who are competent to give or sell, and that, when the parenthood is due to any other cause, a gift or a sale is not permitted. In the case of adoptive parents this natural cause is wanting; and, hence, they cannot give away

1. Śāstradīpikā p. 510

the adopted son again in adoption. In ordinary sonship there is a natural element present; whereas, the sonship of an adopted son is a pure creation of the Śāstras. So, an adoption is possible only in a case where it is allowed by the Śāstras; and, as there is an invisible element involved, we must strictly follow the letters of the texts. Therefore, if a particular time or a particular person is selected or recommended by the texts, our assumption should be that the transaction will be invalid if it is not made at that time or by that person.

PARYUDĀSA

Some writers have made elaborate discussions to determine the exact character of the text :

'न त्वेवैकं पुत्रं दद्यात् प्रतिगृह्णीयाद् वा ।'

Dr. J.N. Bhattacharya regards this text as a 'paryudāsa'. 'If the parents', he says : 'possessed any natural right in their children, then the prohibition could be treated as a prohibition proper; for, there can be a prohibition with regard to only such an act as might be done out of natural power of impulse. But, if it is admitted that the parents have no natural right, then the conclusion is unavoidable that the prohibition with regard to the gift of an only son is a 'paryudāsa'.[1] Now, it may be asked, what would be the difference in effect between a prohibition proper and a 'paryudāsa' ? Exactly the same question has been discussed in the

1. Bhattacharya's Hindu Law p. 175

Adhikaraṇa dealing with the passage : 'न कलञ्जं भक्षयेत्'.[1] It has been decided there that if the passage is regarded as a 'paryudāsa'(viz.,eat everything excepting 'kalañja') a violation of the exception will not cause sin; but, if the passage is regarded as a prohibition proper, sin will be committed on violation. Similarly, in the case before us, if the rule be regarded as an exception, viz., 'give a son other than an only son', the gift of an only son will produce no sin; but, if it is regarded as a prohibition proper, viz., 'do not give an only son', the gift of an only son will produce a sin (which will vitiate the adṛṣṭa element).

The Mīmāṁsakas regard a negative clause as a 'paryudāsa' only when there is either of the two following obstacles standing in the way of regarding the prohibition as a prohibition proper. Where the leading clause in a certain connection is a direction for the performance of some positive duties and there is a subordinate negative clause regarding the non-performance of some of these acts, the negative clause is not to be regarded as a prohibition proper, but as a 'paryudāsa' (exception). In such a case the leading clause indicates that the whole matter is of a positive character. So, if any negative clause comes under it, it seems to be a revolting element. To avoid this difficulty the Mīmāṁsakas take it as a 'paryudāsa'. Again, when by construing a negative rule as a prohibition proper an option becomes inevitable, it is construed as a 'paryudāsa'. An option means two different alternative

1. Mīmāṁsādhikaraṇa VI. ii. 5

courses. When all commands are supposed to proceed from the same authority it is not desirable that there should be commands of a contrary nature. Hence, options are generally repulsive to the Mīmāṁsakas and they try to avoid them by all means. So, if a prohibition is likely to give rise to an option, they try to convert it into a 'paryudāsa', or an exception to the first injunction. These two are the only causes which necessitate the conversion of a prohibition into a 'paryudāsa'. We give below two typical, undisputed instances of 'paryudāsa' and compare the prohibition of the gift of an only son with them. The first instance is **'नेक्षेतोद्यन्तमादित्यम्'**[1] 'do not see the sun rising'. This prohibitory clause is found in the midst of the details of Prajāpati-vrata. Here, the leading clause enjoins the observance of a particular vow which requires the carrying out of some positive details that are mentioned in the subordinate clauses under it. This negative clause cannot be taken apart from the rest, as it is clearly laid down in that particular connection. So, the Śāstradīpikā says :

> **'उपक्रमे श्रुतं कर्मवाचि व्रतपदं यतः। तदन्वयबलात् कर्मविशेषोऽप्यत्र चोद्यते ॥ तेन लक्षणयाप्यत्र पर्युदासः।'**

'As the word, 'vrata' denoting a duty is mentioned in the beginning (the leading clause), and with reference to that a particular duty is enjoined by it (the subordinate clause), it is a case of 'paryudāsa' even by implication'. The negative clause must be construed

---

1. Mīmāṁsādhikaraṇa IV. i. 3

with reference to the positive leading clause; and, so, it cannnot be allowed to retain its negative character. But, this principle does not apply to the case of the gift of an only son; for, the negative clause 'न त्वेवैकं' etc. does not stand under any leading clause imposing any positive duty.

Our second instance is 'यजतिषु येयजामहं करोति, नाऽनुयाजेषु 'in all sacrificial offerings a particular mantra is to be uttered—not in the 'anuyāja' offerings.' Here, the second portion, which is a negative clause, prohibits the uttering of the mantra in certain offerings which the first portion enjoins. The uttering of a particular formula cannot be the outcome of any natural impulse. So, the prescription as well as the prohibition are made here by the sacred texts. Hence, an option arises. To avoid this unpleasant result the prohibition is regarded as an exception. The Śāstradīpikā summarises the case thus :

'यत एव विकल्पोऽयं प्रतिषेधे प्रसज्यते ।
अतस्तत्परिहाराय पर्युदासाश्रयो वरम् ॥'[1]

'An option arises if it is regarded as a prohibition; so, in order to avoid it, it is better to have recourse to a 'paryudāsa'.

Mr. K. L. Sarker has cited a case from Raghunandana's Digest which we may discuss here for the better understanding of the difference between a prohibition and an exception.

1. Adhikarana X. viii. 1

The text discussed by Raghunandana is : 'The 'pārvaṇa-śrāddha' must be performed during the new moon, but not in the night.' Here, the expression 'but not in the night', forms an exception (paryudāsa). Suppose, a man performs the śrādh during the new moon, but in the night. The effect is that he gets no benefit from the performance of the śrādh. But, he commits no positive sin'.[1] No man feels any natural impulse to perform a śrādh. The direction for its performance is obtained from the Smṛti texts.

The texts at first enjoin that it should be performed during the new moon but prohibits its performance in the night. There is no question here of any negative clause standing in the midst of a roll of positive duties. We are only to ascertain whether there is any likelihood of an option taking place. If the performance in the hours of the night is supposed to be enjoined by the texts, its prohibition will bring about an option; but, if it is supposed to be depending on the performer's sweet will, there will be no conflict between the texts, and the prohibition will be regarded as a prohibition proper. Raghunandana and the author of the Karmapradīpa[2] think that the idea of the performance in the night is obtained from the Śāstras; and, hence, they conclude that the prohibition is an exception to the injunction. The author of the Karmapradīpa is of the opinion that, as the performance of an excepted act does not produce any sin, no sin will be committed by

1. Mīmāṁsā Rules p. 333
2. Nārāyaṇācārya

performing a śrādh in the night of the new moon. But, the Mīmāṁsakas think otherwise. The principle has been discussed in the Bhāṭṭadīpikā in connection with the injunction 'न प्रथमयज्ञे प्रवृञ्ज्यात्'[1]. According to it, the period of the new moon may have been fixed by the text but the selection of a particular hour depends on the will of the performer. So, this prohibition is not directed against the injunction of performance but against the independent exercise of the will of the performer. Hence, in the opinion of the Mīmāṁsakas the prohibition is a case of prohibition proper.

Dr. Bhattacharya wants to assert that as the father has no natural proprietary right, it is not possible for him to make the gift of a son at his sweet will. The idea of making such a gift is derived only from the sacred texts; and, if the texts once prescribe such a gift and again prohibit it, an option is sure to arise. To avoid that option it is necessary to have recourse to a 'paryudāsa'. But, those who admit that parents have a natural right even to an only son cannot say that the gift should take place in pursuance of any Śāstric injunction; for, according to them, it depends on the will of parents; and, an injunction is not necessary for the exercise of one's free will. They will regard the passage 'तस्य मातापितरौ प्रभवतः' 'his parents are competent' as declaratory of the natural right of parents, and not as enjoining the gift of a son. The fact that the verb has been used in the indicative mood 'प्रभवतः' and not in the imperative mood also shows that there is no

1. Adhikaraṇa III. iii. 12

command. So, according to them, the prohibition is to be regarded as a prohibition proper and not an exception. A prohibition which stands for checking a natural inclination is never regarded as an exception; otherwise, the clause 'न कलञ्जं भक्षयेत्' would not be a case of prohibition. So, if the present case be treated as a 'paryudāsa', a contradiction of the 'kalañja' maxim would be inevitable. Thus, it is clear that if the natural right of parents is admitted, no modification of the prohibitory force of the passage, 'न त्वेवैकं पुत्रं' etc., will be possible by regarding it as a 'paryudāsa'.

In short, the passage, 'शुक्रशोणितसम्भवः etc.,' cannot be treated as an injunction if the natural right of parents is admitted. It can at best be treated either as a recommendation for making a gift or as a declaration of the existence of such a right. In the former case, the negative clause, 'नैकपुत्रं etc;' will be a prohibition; and, in the latter, it will indicate the want of the existence of natural right. The negative particle must denote a contradiction of what is conveyed by the affirmative passage; otherwise, what is the good of using it at all ?

It may be asked that if the affirmative sentence merely recommends the making of a gift, the negative clause should indicate a mere moral admonition and not a direct prohibition. But, in the present case it is not possible. We have said above that a prohibition which tends to check the natural inclination of a man cannot but be a prohibition proper. Here, the existence of natural right is admitted; so, the prohibition must be a prohibition proper. Besides, we gain nothing by regarding it as a moral admonition. If the affirmative clause were a recommendation, it would necessarily imply an option. What would then be the necessity for conveying the same idea by using another clause? Thus, our conclusion is that the negative clause is a prohibition. In the Mīmāṁsā we find a passage which supports this conclusion: 'आपद्ग्रहणाद्दानापदि न देयः, दातुरयं प्रतिषेधः'. Here, the word 'प्रतिषेधः' is used, and not 'पर्युदास' or any other word. This shows that in the opinion of Vijñāneśvara also these negative clauses are prohibitions, and nothing else.

Now, if it be not admitted that parents have a natural right to their children it will not be possible to hold that one can make a gift of one's son if one so likes. So, a sanction must be obtained from the Śāstras. In this view, the passage: 'तस्य प्रदानविक्रयौ' etc. might be regarded as a general rule prescribing the gift of an only son or any other son. So, the negative clause 'न त्वेवैकं' etc. might become a 'paryudāsa'. But, the passage 'शुक्रशोणितसम्भवः etc.' in the very beginning of the section clearly indicates the existence of a natural right; and, so, the negative clause, also, must stand with reference to the same thing. This clause is, therefore, intended to prohibit the exercise of a natural right. Hence, as we have shown before, it must be regarded as a prohibition proper, and not as a 'paryudāsa'.

Mr.V.N. Mandalik and other writers are of the opinion that the passage: 'न त्वेवैकं ···' is nothing more than a mere 'arthavāda'. But, a negative clause can be regarded as an 'arthavāda' only when it is neither a prohibition nor a 'paryudāsa'. This question arose with regard to the negative text 'न सोमे' (do not perform the offerings in Soma sacrifices) and it has been decided that it is a case of 'arthavāda'. The following is a translation of the portion of the Śāstradīpikā[1] which contains the discussion : 'If the 'ājyabhāga' offerings were available in the Soma sacrifice owing to any injunction or the rule of transference, it would be a case of prohibition. If the injunction of the performance of 'ājyabhāga' offerings were for the sake of Soma-sacrifice as well as for sacrifices other than the Soma, then an exception might be made out of the form 'non-Soma'. The conclusion is that as 'ājyabhāga' offerings are not to be made in the Soma sacrifice, so also they are not to be performed in the Paśu-sacrifice.

So, the clause 'न सोमे' comes to be an 'arthavāda', i.e., a mere statement of a known fact. In pursuance of this conclusion, a negative clause which is neither a prohibition nor a 'paryudāsa', is regarded as an 'arthavāda'. But, we have shown above that the text 'न त्वेवैकं……' is a case of prohibition proper; and, hence, we cannot regard it as an 'arthavāda'. The Adhikaraṇa, referred to above, is called the Niṣedhārthavādādhikaraṇa; and, a negative clause can be regarded as an 'arthavāda' only in accordance with the principle laid down in it. But, it is strange that Mr. Mandalik and others have not at all depended upon this Adhikaraṇa. They have, on the other hand, derived support from the Hetuman-nigadādhikaraṇa.[2] So, we propose to see

1. Śāstradīpikā X. 8. 2
2. Mīmāṁsādhikaraṇa I. ii. 3

how they have applied the principle of the latter Adhikaraṇa to the present case.

THE HETUMAT MAXIM

We quote below an extract from Mr. Mandalik's Hindu Law which will show how he has explained and applied the principle laid down in the Hetuman-nigadādhikaraṇa :

'This text on the most approved principles of criticism must also be treated as a recommendatory one, inasmuch as it contains a precept that is intended for a certain specified purpose. It is a rule of the Pūrva-Mīmāṁsā that all texts supported by the assigning of a reason are to be deemed not as 'vidhi' but simply as 'arthavāda' (recommendatory). When a text is treated as an 'arthavāda', it follows that it has no obligatory force whatsoever. Śabara Svāmin constructs an Adhikaraṇa (a topic) on this head, which he calls Hetuman-nigadādhikaraṇa (a topic in regard to texts which contain a clause containing the reason of the precept) out of five sūtras of Jaimini, Ch I, quarter II, 26-30, and which he begins as follows :

'अथ ये हेतुमन्निगदा :—'शूर्पेण जुहोति, तेन ह्यन्नं क्रियते'—इत्येवमादयः। तेषु सन्देहः, किं स्तुतिस्तेषां कार्यमुत हेतुः ? !

Translation : Now in regard to such 'nigadas' (texts) having clause assigning as reason, as 'one should sacrifice by means of 'śūrpa' (a winnowing basket); for by means of that food is prepared', a doubt arises as to whether they are simply commendatory or contain a reason (making them obligatory). His final reply to the query is 'तस्माद् हेतुमन्निगदस्यापि स्तुतिरेव कार्यम्'. Translation : 'Therefore, the import of texts having a clause that contains a reason is commendation only.'[1] Prof. Keith has also expressed a similar opinion as will appear from the following lines quoted from his book entitled the Karma-Mīmāṁsā :

'The same maxim, however, has been interpreted as supporting the general rule that an injunction for which a reason is adduced is merely equivalent to an 'arthavāda', so that Vaśiṣṭha's rule against the adoption of an only son is reduced to a pious expression of opinion, because it is followed by the explanation that a son is one who saves from hell his natural father, a fact which makes the adoption of an only son undesirable'.[2]

But, Dr. Bhattacharya is against accepting this view. His view will appear from his own words quoted below :

'The argument on which Mr. Mandalik and his followers lay the greatest stress is that founded on the reason assigned in Vaśiṣṭha's text. The Rishi says that an only son should not be given because he is for the perpetuation of lineage. Applying to this the Hetuman-nigadādhikaraṇa as he calls it, Mr. Mandalik arrives at the conclusion that the prohibition as to the adoption of an only son has no legal force. But his reading of the adhikaraṇa is inaccurate; and not only is his translation of it misleading, but his conclusion does not follow from his premises.

---

1. Mandalik's Hindu Law, pp. 499-500
2. Karma-Mīmāṁsā, p. 100

Rules, which contain recommendatory clauses, are, no doubt, generally optional. But, no one who has the least knowledge of the subject would say that they are always so. The संयोगपृथक्त्वन्याय explained in p. 61 ante, clearly shows that a rule or law may contain a recommendatory clause and yet be absolutely binding'.[1]

But, we do not understand how Dr. Bhattacharya applies the two principles simultaneously. In the Hetumannigadādhikaraṇa the 'saṁyogapṛthaktva' maxim forms the basis of the pūrva-pakṣa. So, in the Nyāyasudhā the passage beginning with 'अथापि' of the Vārttika is introduced with these remarks : हेत्वर्थवादसमुच्चयेनायं पूर्वपक्षः, न केवलहेतुत्वेन ।[2] 'This pūrva-pakṣa assumes both reason and commendation and not reason only.' This prima facie conclusion has certainly been given up in arriving at the final conclusion. So, it is not reasonable to assert, on the ground of 'saṁyoga-pṛthaktva' maxim, that there are both a reason as well as a commendation. As it has been decided in the case of the passage, 'तेन ह्यन्नं क्रियते', that it is a mere commendation, so in the passage under discussion, we shall find a commendation only and no injunction. So, the attempt, made by Dr. Bhattacharya, for supporting the existence of an injunction by applying the saṁyoga-pṛthaktva maxim even after admitting that it is a case of Hetumannigadādhikaraṇa, has not been a well-considered one.

---

1. Bhattacharya's Hindu Law, pp. 177-78a
2. Nyāyasudhā p. 83

Dr. Bhattacharya observes: 'The texts which prohibit the adoption of an only son are negative injunctions, which must be treated as exceptional clauses in the texts that enjoin adoption by sonless persons, and not as independent precepts. If they were really independent precepts of an optional nature, then a sonless person could either adopt or not adopt an only son as he pleased'. Dr. Bhattacharya adduces this argument; because, he has all along treated the negative clause as a 'paryudāsa'. But, we have discussed this question at great length and have shown that it is a negative injunction and not a 'paryudāsa'. So, we are unable to attach any weight to this argument. Let us, next, see how Mr. K. L. Sarkar has dealt with this matter. His view will be found in the lines quoted below :

'Some argue, as I already stated, that the statement of a reason vitiates the 'vidhi' in support of which the reason is stated. If this were so, then, in the present case, not only the exception would go out, but even the general rule laying down the power of the parents to give away their sons. I have shown to you that there is no valid basis for the proposition that the statement of a reason vitiates a rule in support of which the reason is stated. I have shown that by the maxim, called 'the Dṛṣṭahetu-Adhikaraṇa', the Adhikaraṇa of the third chapter of the first book of Jaimini, a corrupt reason invalidates a 'vidhi' and not an indifferent far less a good reason. I have also shown to you that by the Hetumannigada-Adhikaraṇa the reason stated is not to be taken as a condition precedent of the 'vidhi', it is to be treated no more than as a mere recital. Thus, the proposition prohibiting the adoption of an only son, cannot be treated as a nullity because a reason is stated for it. The question, however, yet remains whether the particular character of the reason stated in this case for the exception does not reduce to a nullity the exception itself. The reason stated is that an only son is required to continue the line of ancestors of the family in which he has been born; this reason is not corrupt reason within the meaning of the Dṛṣṭahetu-Adhikaraṇa.'[1]

Mr.Mandalik has said that, according to the Hetumat maxim, all texts supported by the assignment of a reason are to be deemed as 'arthavāda's, and Mr. K. L. Sarkar comes to a conclusion that the view (of Mr. Mandalik) is not correct because the Dṛṣṭahetu maxim is not applicable to all such cases. One may like to know if there is any connection between the two principles. It can by no means be said that, according to the Hetumannigada maxim, only those texts should be treated as 'arthavāda's to which corrupt reasons are assigned. In the example, 'शूर्पेण जुहोति, तेन ह्यन्नं क्रियते ।', a connection is established between the winnowing basket and the act of offering; and, the instrumentality of the basket, so far as food is concerned, is required to be assigned as its reason. Because 'śūrpa' is instrumental in preparing food; it is, therefore, that the offerings are to be made with it. One will at once notice that this is no earthly reason at all. So, it must be admitted that this case is not fit for the application of the Dṛṣṭahetu maxim. Hence, if Mr. Sarkar is of opinion that the Hetumannigada

1. K. L. Sarkar's Mīmāṁsā Rules pp. 453-4

maxim applies to those cases only where the reasons are known to be corrupt, we shall not be able to support him. The Dṛṣṭahetu maxim is cited only in those cases where the authoritativeness (प्रामाण्य) of a particular text is in question; but, it is never cited in a case where we are to determine whether a particular text is a 'vidhi' or an 'arthavāda'. The two cases do not touch each other. Hence, it is not reasonable to hold that the difficulty, which was caused by an application of the Hetumannigada maxim, can be removed by avoiding the application of the Dṛṣṭahetu maxim. Thus, we see that the arguments adduced by Dr. Bhattacharya and Mr. K. L. Sarkar for refuting the view of Mr. Mandalik are not sufficient and that the view of Mr. Mandalik remains still uncontroverted.

Yet, we are not prepared to follow Mr. Mandalik. In the first place we must ascertain to which text Mr. Mandalik applies the Hetumat maxim. Does he mean to show that the text 'न त्वेकं etc., is an 'arthavāda', or that the text 'स हि सन्तानाय' etc, is so ? To the former, the maxim cannot apply; for, it does not contain any word denoting reason. In the example cited in the Adhikaraṇa itself, the text 'तेन ह्यन्नं क्रियते', which contains the word हि forms the matter for discussion and not the text 'शूर्पेण जुहोति'. In the second text the word 'हि' is there no doubt but we must know one thing more. It has been clearly propounded in the Bhāṣya that the inevitability of an option is the only bar to accepting the reason. If the fact that the 'śūrpa' is an instrument for preparing food is the cause of its being used as a sacrificial instrument, any article, e. g., a ladle, a pot, or a pan, which is an instrument for preparing food, may be used as an instrument for offering oblations at our option; and, then, the use of the 'śūrpa' which is mentioned in the creative injunction will not be compulsory. Dr. Bhattacharya explains this clearly in the following lines : 'The result of the Hetumannigadādhikaraṇa is that the reason given cannot be taken to extend the scope of the text, so as to support the doctrine that not only the winnowing basket but all the other instruments for preparing rice have to be used also. It is a general principle of interpretation that one 'utpatti-vidhi', or original injunction of the Śāstras, must always be taken to be so worded that there may be no mistake as to its meaning; and, the words used in it must, therefore, be taken in their usual sense without extending or narrowing their meaning. A reason given in support of one 'utpatti-vidhi' cannot be treated as a reason when such a view may affect the interpretation of the text. In such a case the reason given must be regarded according to Śabara Svāmin as having for its object only śruti or commendation.,[1] So, we see that in the case of the 'śūrpa', the only apprehension is that if many articles are regarded as fit to be instruments for offering oblations, an option must take place which will reduce the strictness of the original injunction. But, the present case is quite a different one; because, here, there is no room for an option. Here, the perpetuation of the lineage is put forward as the reason for not making the gift. Any son and particularly an eldest son may be regarded as able to

1. Bhattacharya, Hindu Law, p. 178

perpetuate the lineage. But, there can be no choice between the gift of an eldest son and that of an only son; for, he who is the father of an eldest son cannot be the father of an only son at the same time. So, there is no possibility of extending the scope of the negative clause by reason of an option.

Thus, it becomes clear that the text **'स हि सन्तानाय पूर्वेषाम्'** does not come within the purview of the Hetumat maxim. So, the passage need not be regarded as an 'arthavāda' but as one containing a reason. But, on the other hand, we do not gain anything by supposing that there is such a reason assigned here as has been indicated above. We may rather suppose that the text **'स हि सन्तानाय पूर्वेषाम्'** is itself an injunction. We have said before that it can be construed in a different way. We can construe it as **'पूर्वेषां स सन्तानाय भवति'**. 'He belongs to his fore-fathers and exists for perpetuation'. In this way the text may be regarded as laying down that the fore-fathers have a right to an only son. This idea is a peculiar one; and, as such, it is fit to be contained in an injunction. Otherwise, what is the good of emphatically asserting a thing (perpetuation of lineage) which is too well-known. This construction is consistent with the previous text which forbids the gift of an only son : an only son must neither be given nor accepted because he is a property of his fore-fathers. In this construction the word **'हि'** is used in its ordinary sense and is not meaningless.

It is not a fact that the Mīmāṁsakas invariably recognise all those texts as 'arthavāda's in which a word denoting a reason is found. For instance, we may take the text 'न ह्यत्र अनुयाजा इज्यन्ते'. 'Because the 'anuyāja' offerings are not to be made here'. The text with reference to which this reason is assigned is 'चतुर्जुह्वां गृह्णाति'. 'Takes the oblation four times in the sacrificial ladle'. Here, the first text states that the non-performance of the 'anuyāja' offerings is the reason for taking the oblation four times. In the Nyāyasudhā it is so explained in the Hetumannigadādhikaraṇa : चतुर् गृहीतानि आज्यानि भवन्ति । न ह्यत्र अनुयाजा इज्यन्ते—इत्यादयः परमार्थहेतवः"[1] The oblations are to be taken four times. The passages न ह्यत्र etc. are true reasons. So, we see that there are passages which are recognised as containing true reasons. It should also be noticed here that the text prohibiting the gift of an only son will remain unaffected even though we recognise the proposition 'स हि सन्तानाय' etc., as an 'arthavāda'. In the case of the 'śūrpa' the proposition 'तेन ह्यन्नं क्रियते' is recognised as an 'arthavāda'; but, the text 'शूर्पेण जुहोति' retains its injunctive character all the same and the use of the 'śūrpa' is compulsory owing to this injunction. So, even an application of the Hetumat maxim will not reduce the negative text into a recommendation. Mr. Mandalik has made an initial mistake in not correctly ascertaining the effect of the application of the Hetumat maxim. He has not looked into the fact that it applies only to the proposition that contains the reason and that its effect is to reduce that text only into an 'arthavāda' or a mere recital. It has been an error on the part of Mr. Mandalik to suppose that it affects any other neighbouring text. Prof. Keith also has committed the same mistake.

---

1. Nyāyasudhā p. 82

We have shown above, that the text 'स हि सन्तानाय' may be treated as an injunction or an 'arthavāda'. The Hetumat maxim is not applicable to this text; but, even if it be taken for granted that the said maxim applies here, there is not the slightest doubt that it will not touch the other text 'नैकं पुत्रं' etc.

MITĀKṢARĀ TEXTS

We find that Mr. Mandalik, Mr. Golap Candra Sarkar and others, have on the authority of the passage, दातुरयं प्रतिषेधः (the prohibition regards the giver) of the Mitākṣarā, come to the conclusion that the adoption of an only son or of an eldest son is valid, because the prohibition affects the giver only and not the adoption. The authority of the Mitākṣarā regarding adoption is respected throughout India and its view is regarded as authoritative. So, we ought to examine here the prohibitory passages of the Mitākṣarā from the Mīmāṁsā point of view.

Those passages are as follow :

'आपद्ग्रहणाद् अनापदि न देयः। दातुरयं प्रतिषेधः।
तथा एकपुत्रो न देयः। तथा अनेकपुत्रसद्भावे ज्येष्ठो न देयः।'

By specifying distress it is intimated that the son should not be given unless there be distress. This prohibition is with regard to the giver. Similarly, an only son should not be given. Similarly, though more than one son exists the first-born should not be given...........

The remark 'दातुरयं प्रतिषेधः' is supplemented in the Bālambhaṭṭi with the words 'न प्रतिग्रहीतुः' 'does not regard the taker'.

'It expressly says' says Mr. Golap Chandra Sarkar 'that the prohibition regards the giver, and necessarily implies that it does not regard the taker, and, therefore, the gift is valid in law'.[1] The Dattaka-mīmāṁsā explains the passage by saying that the taker also is implied by it. The first view is that if the prohibited gift is made, the giver will commit a sin; whereas, according to the second view, the sin will affect the taker also. But, neither of the two views indicates that the adoption will be invalid. It is for this reason that the passage is quoted in the Mayūkha with the remark, 'न क्रत्वर्थः'. If this prohibition is not क्रत्वर्थं it may be पुरुषार्थं, as the two terms are usually contrary. A prohibition is regarded as 'puruṣārtha' in a case where the commission of the prohibited act even during the performance of a sacrifice does not vitiate the result of the sacrifice but separately gives rise to a sin; whereas, in a case of 'kratvartha' prohibition, the commission of the prohibited act at the time of the sacrifice will spoil the result.[2] So, the opinion of the author of the Mitākṣarā appears to be that the performance of a gift or an acceptance for effecting an adoption, even in a case where it is prohibited will give rise to a sin but will not make the adoption invalid.

It may appear, according to the view stated above, that all prohibited cases of adoption are valid, because the violation of a prohibition may render one's act improper but not invalid. But, in fact, it is not so. In a case of prohibition we are to judge as to what particular point the prohibition is directed. In the above

1. Law of Adoption p. 287
2. Mīmāṁsādhikaraṇa IV. i. 1

case a restriction is imposed with regard to the proper time for adoption, and its result concerns only the agent; but, in a case where a restriction is made with regard to the object of the gift, a violation will make the adoption invalid. As an example we can take the next item, viz., the case of the adoption of an only son. Here, the prohibition is in respect of an only son who is the object of the gift; and, hence, the adoption of an only son will be invalid. The word **'तथा'** is used twice in the above extract and is meant to connect the three prohibitions that are derived by the author of the Mitākṣarā by combining the texts of Yājñavalkya and Vaśiṣṭha. The three prohibitions respectively are **'अनापदि न देयः'**, **'एकपुत्रो न देयः'** and **'ज्येष्ठपुत्रो न देयः'**. Besides these three, the word **'तथा'** does not connect anything else. Therefore, the expression **'दातुरयं प्रतिषेधः'** has no forward reference. So, the exact meanings of the three clauses would be—a son is to be given only in time of distress, even in time of distress one who is not an only son is to be given, one who is not the eldest son is to be given. But, it is to be noticed that all these prohibitions are not of the same character. If a father gives away his son when there is no distress, it qualifies the giver (the giver who is in distress). But, if an only son is not an object of gift the prohibition attaches to the son and not to the father. The same argument applies to the case of the eldest son also. So, when it is said that somethiug is not to be given we can make a distinction between two sets of cases. Where the prohibition affects the giver the adoption will be improper but not invalid; but, where the prohibition regards the object of the gift the adoption will be invalid.

'The first rule', says Mr. Golap Chandra Sarkar, 'is undoubtedly one of moral obligation, for it expressly says that the prohibition regards the giver, and necessarily implies that it does not regard the taker and, therefore, the gift is valid in law.' We can, as we have shown above, accept this conclusion as correct. But, we are unable to conform to the view of the learned author as expressed in the extract quoted below: 'It follows, therefore, that the second prohibition is a rule of the same character as the first, for in no other respect can there be a similarity between them. And, for the same reason, the third rule also must be of the same description.[1] As regards these remarks of Mr. Sarkar we must say that they do not rest on a strong basis. It must not be forgotten that the above three clauses of the Mitākṣarā (अनापद्रि न देयः etc.,) are not prohibitions imposed by the author of the Mitākṣarā; but, they are simply the statements of the prohibitions implied by the text of Yājñavalkya, combined with other texts. So, these three clauses represent the corresponding negative sides of the three restrictive injunctions which are derived by combining the texts, viz., the gift is to be made only in distress, one other than an only son is to be given and one other than the eldest son is to be given. The negative counterpart of a restrictive injunction is a prohibition proper. So, the three negative clauses of the Mitākṣarā are prohibitions proper. It is a well-settled conclusion with the Mīmāṁsakas that if an act, which is prohibited by an implied prohibition, is performed, the action will not produce the desired result. To illustrate this rule, we may cite the injunction 'व्रीहीनवहन्ति' 'Husk the barley-corn', which has been

1. Law of Adoption, p. 287

discussed under the Sūtra 'तानि द्वैधं गुणप्रधानकर्माणि'[1] and which is regarded as a typical case of restrictive injunction. According to this injunction the sacrificer is required to remove the chaff by husking. It has been held that if the sacrificer adopts any other process for removing the chaff, such as picking out the grains with the nails of the hands, etc., the grains will not be fit for use in the sacrifice; and, consequently, the whole performance will be defective and will not produce the desired result. It cannot be said that the grains are grains and it does not matter whether we take them out by the one process or the other; for, the very function of a restrictive injunction is to restrict our choice. Had the alternative courses that are excluded by a restrictive injunction been still open to us, there would have been no necessity for recognising a particular class of injunctions as restrictive injunctions in the Mīmāṁsā. There is not the slightest doubt that the Mitākṣarā treats the above texts of Yājñavalkya and Vaśiṣṭha as giving restrictive injunctions; and, so, if an adoption does not take place strictly in accordance with the injunctions, it will be invalid.

But, another thing, also, is to be taken into consideration. Restictive injunctions may be divided into two classes—kratvartha and puruṣārtha. The example 'व्रीहीनवहन्ति' illustrates the former, and the example 'प्राङ्मुखोऽन्नानि भुञ्जीत', 'at the time of taking meals sit with your face towards the east', illustrates the latter. We have said before that a violation of an

1. II. i. 6

injunction of the former class spoils a sacrifice, whereas a violation of an injunction of the other description, produces some unseen demerit in the agent.[1] Now, if the prohibition 'आपदि न देयः' of the Mitākṣarā is regarded as puruṣārtha, its corresponding restrictive injunction 'अनापदि एव देयः' must also be regarded as puruṣārtha. The consequence will be that the act of giving, whether it is performed in times of distress or not, will simply concern the giver and not the validity of the adoption. But, we have shown at the outset that all the texts clearly state that दान produces दत्तकत्व and not any other unseen merit; and, therefore, it cannot be said that the act of giving has nothing to do with the validity of adoption. So, a contradiction takes place. The only means of avoiding this contradiction is to admit that the gift is both 'kratvartha' and 'puruṣārtha'. The effect of this will be that the gift will not only concern the giver but the validity of adoption also. But, if we admit that the injunction relating to gift is both 'kratvartha' and 'puruṣārtha', we must at the same time admit that its corresponding prohibition 'अनापदि न देयः' (which is stated in the Mitākṣarā), is also both 'kratvartha' and 'puruṣārtha'. The observation of the Mayūkha, 'न क्रत्वर्थः' may be explained as not 'kratvartha' only but 'puruṣārtha' also.

According to this view, if a son is given when there is no distress, the adoption will be invalid. Similarly, the adoption of an only son or of an eldest son will be invalid. Mr. Golap Chandra Sarkar has taken a good deal of trouble to show that by the word, 'तथा' Vijñā-

1. Nyāyaratnamālā

neśvara means nothing but similarity. The word can denote similarity if the view just expressed above, is accepted; but, the result will be exactly the reverse of what Mr. Sarkar has propounded.

Let us summarise here the conclusions of the above discussions. From the statements of the Mitākṣarā two views may be gathered. The first is that even in a case where the gift and the acceptance are prohibited, the adoption may be valid if the prohibition regards the giver only; but, it will not be valid if the prohibition regards the object of the gift. The second view is that even where the prohibition regards the giver only, the adoption will be invalid. So, we see that though there may be a dispute regarding the validity of the adoption of a child given at a time when there is no distress, the invalidity of the adoption of an only son is quite undisputed.
